W9-CTN-828

TOP to BOTTOM

DOWN UNDER

TED and BETSY LEWIN

Lee & Low Books Inc. *New York*

To James Doherty,

Vice President and General Curator of Wildlife,
Wildlife Conservation Society/Bronx Zoo,
for kindly sharing his knowledge
and offering thoughtful suggestions

Copyright © 2005 by Ted and Betsy Lewin
All rights reserved. No part of this book may be reproduced, transmitted, or stored in
an information retrieval system in any form or by any means, electronic, mechanical,
photocopying, recording, or otherwise, without written permission from the publisher.

LEE & LOW BOOKS Inc., 95 Madison Avenue, New York, NY 10016, leeandlow.com
Hardcover edition published in 2005 by HarperCollins Children's Books

Cover/series design by Paul Colin, Cezanne Studio
Book production by The Kids at Our House
Interior typography by Carla Weiss; the text is set in Egyptienne
The full-color illustrations are rendered in watercolor on Strathmore Bristol board
Manufactured in China by South China Printing Co., July 2014
10 9 8 7 6 5 4 3 2 1
First LEE & LOW BOOKS Edition, 2014

Library of Congress Cataloging-in-Publication Data
Lewin, Ted. Top to bottom down under / Ted & Betsy Lewin. — 1st ed.   p. cm.
Summary: Ted and Betsy Lewin share their adventures while traveling in northern
and southern Australia, describing the wildlife and landscapes they encounter.
ISBN 978-1-62014-184-7 (paperback)
1. Australia—Description and travel—Juvenile literature. 2. Natural history—
Australia—Juvenile literature. 3. Lewin, Ted—Journeys—Australia—Juvenile literature.
4. Lewin, Betsy—Journeys—Australia—Juvenile literature. [1. Australia—Description
and travel. 2. Animals—Australia. 3. Natural history—Australia.] I. Lewin, Betsy. II. Title.
DU105.2.L49 2005   919.4—dc22   2003026934

FSC
www.fsc.org
MIX
Paper from
responsible sources
FSC® C101537

Australian slang*

bonzer—*great*

fair dinkum—*genuine*

holy dooley—*good grief*

tucker—*food*

Look for these words inside.

Galahs and emu

Kakadu National Park

AUSTRALIA

Kangaroo Island

United States
Australia

In Australia, there's a furry little animal that has a bill like a duck and a tail like a beaver. It has venom like a snake and lays eggs like a bird. There's a bird that lives in a hole like a mole and swims like a fish, but it can't fly. There are animals that hop on feet nearly the size of skateboards and carry their babies in their pockets. There are lizards that run on two feet like a human, and crocodiles, called salties, with teeth like a *T. rex*. Some of these animals are found nowhere else on Earth. We've come more than halfway around the world to see them.

At the Top

We're here, at last, in the "land down under," so called because Australia lies below the equator in the southern hemisphere. On the way, we lost a whole day in the middle of the ocean, crossing the international dateline. And the seasons are reversed. It's fall here, and springtime at home.

Australia is so large from top to bottom that it's hot in the north and cold in the south. It's also said that when you flush the toilet, the water swirls down in the opposite direction than it does in the northern hemisphere. (It doesn't.)

Now that we're totally confused, we leave for Kakadu National Park, one of the wildest, most remote, most beautiful places anywhere. The aboriginal people of the Alligator River region have inhabited this area for more than 30,000 years. That's more than 25,000 years before the pyramids were built in Egypt. The park is 7,453 square miles, the size of Connecticut.

At the campground, we set up our tent next to the DANGER. CROCODILES. WATCH YOUR CHILDREN AND DOGS sign. We curl up in our sleeping bags, not sure what day it is, or time of year, or why crocodiles eat only children and dogs. We are resting up for our first trip to a billabong.

Yellow Water Billabong

Our skiff glides out into Yellow Water Billabong, a backwater lagoon. The aboriginal word "billa" means water. The "bong" part is anybody's guess. The tiny, yellow snowflake lilies that carpet the water in the wet season give this billabong its name.

Islands of Pandanus palms, freshwater mangroves, and tall paperbark gum trees fill the landscape. Jabiru storks, five feet tall, and plumed ducks stand guard.

We search the banks for big salties, remembering not to drag our fingers in the water. Don't let the word "salty" fool you. Salties, or estuarine crocodiles, can live in the fresh water of a billabong as well as in salt water.

Fishermen pass in search of the giant barramundi, a fish that can weigh up to two hundred pounds.

A lotus bird looks as if it is walking on water. Actually it's walking on lily pads. If its chicks are threatened, the male lotus bird scoops them up under his wings and carries them to safety.

Finally, we see a big salty the same color as the bank. It's about fifteen feet long, bigger than our skiff. Its entire body rests on the bank except for its nose, which is underwater. The croc, neither moving nor breathing, has "shut down."

A crocodile can maintain a heart rate of only three to five heartbeats per minute for an hour or more.

On land, salties can run as fast as fifteen miles per hour. So, if a salty chases you, run either *sixteen* miles an hour or in a zigzag fashion. Salties can't turn fast because of their tails. *Never* run in a straight line, especially at fourteen miles per hour.

We go deeper into the paperbark swamp. The water is choked with soft, green weeds. A croc caught a thirty-pound barramundi and held on to it for two days until it rotted. Now the croc lurches half its length out of the water, shaking its head violently from side to side. SPLASH! Chunks of rotten fish go flying. We're soaked and stinking of fish.

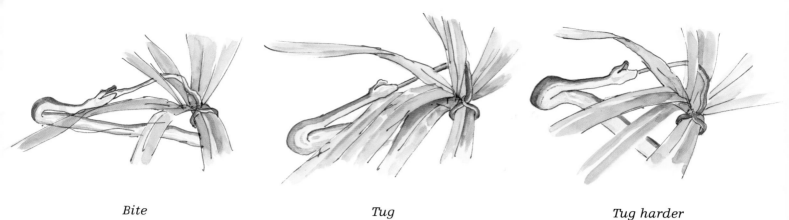

Bite   *Tug*   *Tug harder*

Time to move on. We see a strange movement in a tree. It's an olive python. Close by, a flycatcher sits calmly on its eggs. The python is swallowing another snake that is lighter in color, but the prey holds on tenaciously to the tree. We watch, spellbound. Finally, the lighter snake lets go and both snakes fall through a thick spiderweb, swinging upside down like a grotesque pendulum. The flycatcher dreamily waits for a new life to appear as another life slips away.

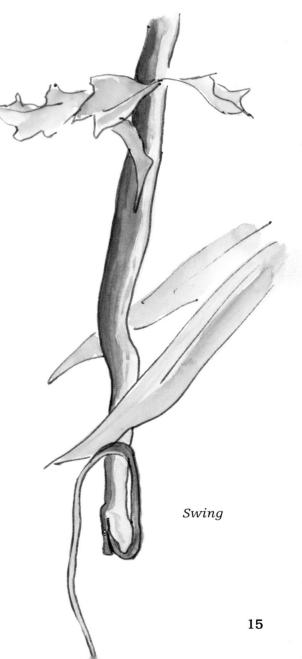

Swing

Dense stands of Pandanus line the banks on their stilt roots. Aboriginals cut the leaves into strips, roll them, and weave them into ditty bags, which they use to carry just about everything.

(ALL CIRCA 1900)

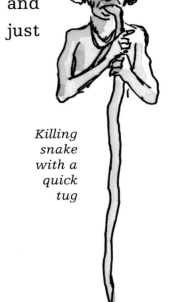

Killing snake with a quick tug

Ditty bag

On a paperbark raft

Watch out! Our skiff has drifted toward a freshwater mangrove, or "itchy" tree. If you come in contact with the grubs on the underside of the leaves, you get itchy all over.

Whoops! A big salty with enormous choppers sits so still we almost miss it. The salty is yellow-green in color, newly arrived from the ocean. The longer crocodiles are away from salt water, the darker their skins become, until they are as dark as the color of the billabong bank.

What a bonzer* croc! A big monitor lizard, called a goanna, swaggers by. Two monsters from the Jurassic era! We start the engine and leave the old fossils to themselves.

*Gathering
water-lily roots*

The landscape ahead turns to Dreamtime. The black water is framed by Pandanus and great, high stands of Arnhem bamboo. No one knows just how the bamboo got here. The aboriginals tell Dreamtime (creation) stories to explain its appearance.

As we sit quietly in this grove of Dreamtime bamboo, we think about how the aboriginal people have always lived in perfect harmony with this land.

A good catch

*Boy with
young salty*

Roping a salty

The next day we leave camp in the cruiser. On either side of the road, vast yellow-brown flood plains are punctuated by blackened, newly burned stretches and bright green growth around water holes. The sky is dark gray, heavy with clouds. A dingo crosses in front of us and lies down in a fresh burn, head flat on the ground. The rest of the pack appears in the tall, green grass. Two whistling kites sit nearby on the rotting carcass of a water buffalo. Other kites circle and wheel in like vultures, trying to buzz them off. A crow joins in the confusion.

Now the dingo nearest us tugs at the buffalo with everything it's got, rips a shred of skin and meat loose, and bolts it down. For five minutes the other dingoes share the carcass.

Suddenly, a ferocious fight breaks out. The dingo near us turns, drops its hindquarters, lays back its ears, and bares its teeth in a hideous grin. The pack attacks, then gives chase when our dingo flees. No one returns to the carcass, not even the crow.

At the Bottom

Now we're flying over the "red center"—mile after mile of wild, empty, red land. We're on our way to Flinders Chase National Park on Kangaroo Island, home to almost all of Australia's wildlife *except* dingoes. Kangaroo Island is a green jewel in the cold Southern Sea, larger than the state of Rhode Island.

In 1802 it was discovered by Captain Matthew Flinders, a young British explorer. Uninhabited then, it now has a population of almost four thousand people.

In the late afternoon sun, kangaroos and Cape Barren geese graze on broad, green meadows. Flightless emus walk by, striking poses with each step, red-eyed and haughty. All are protected and unafraid of humans.

A Kangaroo Island kangaroo and the tiny joey in her pouch graze the short grass. It's as if Mama has two heads. The kangaroos on Kangaroo Island are darker, stockier, shorter limbed, and slower moving than the kangaroos on the mainland.

25

Hmmm.

Boink!

Yum!

Koalas hang in the tops of the rough bark manna gums like great bunches of soft, furry fruit. One tiny chocolate brown baby clings to its mother between her belly and the tree. Koala means "no drink" in the aboriginal language.

That evening, as we eat our rice laced with Tabasco sauce, four kangaroos and a brush-tailed possum invite themselves to dinner. The possum sits on our plates. Mama kangaroo intercepts our food on its way to our mouths. Another grabs our shirtfronts and rocks back onto her tail, freeing up her very strong, clawed feet—feet that could kick your guts out. She can *have* our tucker.* No worries!

Early explorers asked the aborigines the name of the "jumping animal." They answered "kangaroo," which means "I don't understand your question."

Holy dooley!*

The next day we spot a little thorn bush walking across the road in broad daylight. An echidna. There are only two kinds of monotremes, or egg-laying mammals, in the world— the echidna and the platypus.

Sensing our presence, the echidna stops and tucks its long nose under its body. Its spiny back prickles in the air as it starts sinking into the ground. We back off, afraid that if it keeps digging it will disappear before our eyes like Rumpelstiltskin. Then, the little thorn bush rises up out of its hole and waddles off into the scrub.

Rocky River is a swift-moving stream full of great gum tree trunks and long, fanlike waterweeds. Moss grows everywhere. It is home to the other egg layer, the platypus.

In the pouring rain we watch the surface for the rush of bubbles that will signal its arrival. Then we realize that water striders send false platypus signals. So do leaves. And raindrops. Finally, at dusk, not five feet from us, a sleek little beaver body and soft leather bill pops to the surface.

When its nictitating membranes are shut, its eyes look like yellow headlights. When its membranes are open, we see little black shiny eyes.

PLOP! The platypus works its way underwater. Perhaps it is probing and nuzzling with its sensitive bill, feeding on insects, grubs, and small fish, storing them in its cheek pouches. It slides up into its burrow and is gone.

What luck! Seeing *both* monotremes in *one* day!

Venomous spur

Webbed foot

Not far down the coast from our campsite, there's an enchanted place called Seal Bay. The beach and surrounding dunes are littered with Australian sea lions sleeping on blankets of black seaweed, silver gulls in attendance.

We walk out on the beach, expecting all the sea lions to flee. Instead, they continue to sleep, scratch, and yawn—wonderful, whiskered creatures smelling of fish and the sea.

A big female galumphs toward us, mouth wide open. Is she greeting us or charging us? She nuzzles, bites, pushes, and barks at every other sea lion on the beach. They look at her wearily, yawn, and lie back as she waddles into the sea.

We lie down on the warm sand in the midst of the herd. Five hundred strong, the sea lions are about ten percent of all their kind that are left in the world. Huge bulls sit as solid as pyramids, noses pointed to the sky, eyes closed, dozing. Two young bulls joust on a field of seaweed. They shoulder, push, and bite each other like puppies. When they tire of the game, they, too, doze off. All this yawning and sleeping is catching. Before long, we are fast asleep too.

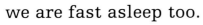

It is dark, very cold, and windy where the fairy penguins live. We pick our way carefully down the jumbled, slippery, lichen-covered rocks to the shore. The sun sets, and the rocks take on monstrous shapes—sea serpents, gigantic toads, and lizards.

Over the sound of the sea breaking on the rocks, we hear yapping and laughing. A crowd of fairy penguins, like little "people" dressed to the nines, waddle out of the sea after a long day of fishing.

It is our last night in this wondrous land. As we nestle into our sleeping bags, we think about the long trip home.

Fall will change back to spring, and we will pick up the day we lost in the middle of the ocean. And now we dream about those little "people" out there in that cold, black sea, laughing their hearts out.

Mates, These Are Fair Dinkum* Facts!

Australian sea lion: It swims with its front flippers and steers with its back flippers. Adult females weigh over 300 pounds. Males weigh over 800 pounds.

Barramundi: "Barramundi" is the aboriginal word for large, scaled fish. There are no young female

barramundi. All are males for the first seven years. Then they turn into females.

Echidna: (Pronounced e-kid'-na). Echidnas have two types of hair: one type for warmth; the other, with long, sharp spikes, for protection. The echidna's nose is sensitive to electrical signals from its prey. The prey is gathered on its long, sticky tongue. A baby echidna, or puggle, suckles inside its mother's pouch. When it develops spines, it is evicted.

Estuarine crocodile: It grows one foot every year for the first seven to ten years, then about an inch a year. A throat flap helps crocodiles to swallow underwater without drowning. The temperature at which crocodile eggs are kept determines the sex of the brood. Warmer temperatures produce all females.

Fairy penguin: At two pounds in weight and ten inches in height, it is the smallest penguin in the world. It can live eighteen to twenty years.

Kangaroo: Males are called boomers, females are flyers, and babies are joeys. Kangaroos travel in groups known as mobs. They are one inch long at birth and never stop growing during their lifetime. They are marsupials, which means that they carry their babies in their pouches.

Koala: Koalas live alone or in pairs, and sometimes in small groups. Males have harems of females. Koalas eat only eucalyptus leaves and shoots, and soil to aid in digestion.

Platypus: A platypus can eat its own body weight in one night. Platypus babies, also called puggles, feed on milk that oozes from pores in the mother's skin. The spurs of the male can deliver enough venom to kill a dog or make a human miserable.

Water buffalo: Introduced into Australia from Southeast Asia, feral buffalo are very destructive to the environment.

W9-CTN-986

Published by The Baltimore Orioles

Copyright 1995 The Baltimore Orioles

All rights reserved

ISBN#0-9648338-0-8

Foreword

BY

JON MILLER

RIGHT AWAY, LET ME POINT OUT, since coming to Baltimore in 1983, I have never broadcast an Orioles game in which Cal Ripken was not the starting shortstop. In fact, it wasn't until late in my fifth season with the Orioles that I even broadcast an inning in which Cal was not the shortstop.

The first time I saw Ripken in spring training that year he was with Mark Belanger, one of the greatest shortstops ever. Belanger had been brought in to teach Cal the fine points of playing short. What Cal was doing was picking Belanger's brain on all the hitters in the league — their tendencies and where he should position himself. I learned then that he was a student of the game.

Of course, back in '83, we didn't think of Cal as an "Iron Man." We just knew that he was very good. And when the Orioles began their typical late season push to the pennant, he was magnificent!

On August 13 of that year, in Chicago, Cal hit a 2-run homer in the 8th inning to break a 2-2 tie as the Orioles won the game, 5-2. That game began a remarkable stretch that saw the Orioles go 34-10 until they clinched the division in September. Cal led the way in that amazing 44-game stretch as he hit .391. It was the greatest stretch of clutch hitting I've ever seen.

Cal always had a lot of respect for his dad and the two were always discussing baseball. Early in the 1984 season, I brought my Strat-O-Matic table-top baseball game on the team's charter flight from Baltimore to the West Coast. Cal and I

ended up playing a series between the Orioles and the Tigers. Cal was the Orioles manager (with Mike Flanagan as pitching coach) and I managed the Tigers. After my Tigers beat his Orioles in the first game, I chided Cal for making some poor managerial decisions (which was true — he used up his bench in the middle of the game). So, Cal took the score sheet from our Strat-O-Matic game and sat with his dad and went over the different managerial decisions he had made. Fifteen minutes later, he came back and said, "I know what I did wrong. Let's play again." That's when I learned, first-hand, that "Junior" doesn't like to lose...at anything. But I also learned again about his desire to always learn more about the game.

A couple of years ago when younger brother Bill Ripken went to Texas, I asked him what he would do if he were heading to second and had to try to take out his brother Cal to prevent a double-play. I mean, it was his own brother and "The Streak" and all. "I'd go hard and try to hurt him!" Billy declared. "In fact," he continued, "I've been waiting my whole life to get him a good one!" Then Billy showed me a small scar on his face and said, "See this? That's from Cal's game 'Sack the Quarterback' when we were kids." It seems the idea of the game was for Billy, as the quarterback, to pick up the football and try to keep from getting annihilated by Cal, who was a foot taller and 50 pounds heavier.

The Ripken saga was starting to look like "East of Eden." Said Billy, "I'm not thinking 'What if it happens?' I'm counting on it happening."

Which is not to say they're not still the best of friends and very close. It's just that the Brothers Ripken seem to share that family legacy of competitiveness. The desire to win.

One Ripken story which I didn't witness, but wish I had, occurred after the 1990 season. Cal was part of a Major League All-Star team that was going to play a series of games in Japan. Both Cal and Ozzie Smith arrived in L.A., a day ahead of the rest of the team, and arranged to work out, just the two of them, at Dodger Stadium.

At one point, each took a fungo bat and gave the other a workout at shortstop. Subtly, Cal decided to test the "Wizard" and see for himself how good the great Ozzie Smith really was. Cal hit some balls right at him, then to his left and then to his right. Then, Cal hit one far to his right and then the next one far to his left. He hit them with short-hops and in-between hops. He hit them hard and he hit slow choppers. Cal worked him so hard that the winded "Wizard" finally shouted, "Enough!"

Imagine that scene. The two greatest shortstops of their era, in fact, two of the greatest shortstops of all-time, giving each other a workout in an empty stadium. And the "Iron Man" put the "Wizard" to the test, to see for himself how good the "Wizard" really was. Said Ripken, "He got to some balls I didn't think he would. I thought he was great...a winning player."

Ah, yes! The essence of Cal Ripken the ballplayer. Doing whatever it takes to win.

Winston Churchill once said, "We cannot guarantee success, we can only deserve it." That's what I think of when I look back at my 13 seasons of watching him play. Not "The Streak," but rather the total dedication. Not playing every day, but being prepared to play every day.

Enjoy this, Cal. You earned it. You deserve it. ■

Table of Contents

Chapter 1
NON-STOP SHORTSTOP 8

In pursuit of Lou Gehrig's consecutive game streak record, Cal Ripken Jr. talks about the streak, what it means to him, and how it has affected his career. By John Delcos.

Chapter 2
OFFENSIVELY SPEAKING 14

Gordon Beard focuses on Cal Ripken's offensive abilities, his amazing numbers over the years, and his constant strive for perfection with the bat.

Chapter 3
RIPKEN: FOR THE DEFENSE 24

Defensively speaking, there is no other shortstop like Cal Ripken Jr. His consistent, intelligent play continues to make him a hometown and national baseball favorite. By Bob Brown.

Chapter 4
BASEBALL'S IRON AGE 32

Ripken and Gehrig. Gehrig and Ripken. What are their similarities, really? Is it just The Streak, or is there more that these two talents share? Mike Gesker points out some unique similarities and differences between the Iron Man and the Iron Horse.

Chapter 5
ALL IN THE FAMILY 46

Baseball is in Cal Ripken Jr.'s blood. Jack Gilden speaks with members of Cal's family about their lives in baseball, major influences on Cal's career, and the roots that make Cal who he is today.

Chapter 6
"BASEBALL GOD" 60

It's a unanimous decision. Those who work with and play baseball with Cal Ripken Jr. every day agree that Cal is special for many reasons. Anthony Verni reports on why Cal's friends, teammates, and co-workers believe he is a player unlike any other in Major League Baseball.

Chapter 7
LOCAL HERO 70

The hometown fans speak out! Fan stories about Cal Ripken Jr. are abundant! Mary Hughes delves into the hometown pool of fans for their best Cal Ripken Jr. story.

Chapter 8
CAREER TIMELINE 80

Since May 20, 1982, when Cal Ripken Jr.'s streak began, much has happened in the world, and in the game of baseball. Look back at Cal's remarkable career in this year-by-year summary.

Appendix
THE CAL SESSIONS 98

The national media has followed Cal Ripken Jr. all season, with questions old and new, from one city to the next. Here are the best of those sessions, along with lists of Cal's standings among his contemporaries.

"I never set out
to do this."

~ Cal Ripken Jr ~

Chapter 1

Non~Stop Shortstop

BY

JOHN DELCOS

IT'S THE BOTTOM OF THE NINTH and Cal Ripken is in scoring position in his pursuit of immortality.

The Streak, as it has become known, has endured the grind that chews up and spits out the greatest of his peers. After 14 spring trainings and cross-country travel, bruises and twisted knees, sprained ankles and the common cold, and just being tired, Ripken is still there—day after day.

He's there because he wants to be, not because he has to be, and to understand that distinction is to understand what motivates this future Hall of Famer. It is this work ethic that we are honoring. It is this that we celebrate.

"[The Streak] is something I'm proud of, but I can honestly say I never put the uniform on once just to continue The Streak," said Ripken, who, on May 30, 1982, unknowingly began his pursuit of Lou Gehrig's record 2,130 consecutive games.

"I never set out to do this. I'm a baseball player, and my father taught me the importance of being in the line-up every day and having your teammates be able to depend on you. To me, this streak is just an extension of my approach and my beliefs."

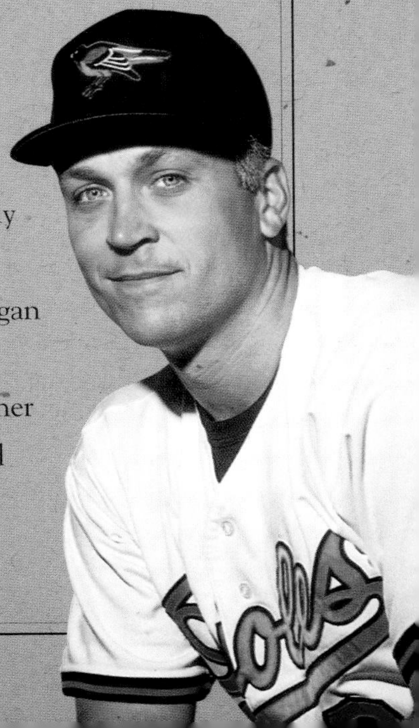

9

After the eight-month layoff, The Streak resumed this season at 2,009 games, 122 shy of Gehrig's unbreakable record. From the moment he arrived in Florida until his destiny—September 6, against the California Angels in Camden Yards—it was the same everywhere.

Every new town, questions about The Streak.

How does he feel about it?

What does it mean to baseball?

Isn't he glad the strike didn't end The Streak?

Was there ever a time when he didn't feel like playing?

Was there a time when he almost didn't play?

Everywhere, questions and attention...the two things Ripken enjoys least about the game he loves.

One more: Is it fair that his career is identified by The Streak?

That last one used to rub him raw, like wearing cleats that are too small.

When Ripken moved past Everett Scott (1,307 games) in 1990, he said it was unfair his career would be defined by The Streak, noting his All-Star appearances and power production.

He didn't mean to do it! But, over the years, Cal's become more comfortable with the idea of The Streak.

Cal Ripken Jr. played parts of 12 seasons with his father in an Orioles uniform as both coach and manager. In fact, Cal Sr. became the first father ever to manage two sons (Bill Ripken) simultaneously during a regular season in major league baseball.

"I think I've shown that I'm a good player, and that I've accomplished other things in my career besides The Streak," Ripken said five summers ago. "I don't think it's fair that people look at me because of this one thing."

But they do. And to Ripken's relief and credit — like adjusting and going to right field when all he gets are pitches on the outside corner — he has accepted his destiny.

"It seems like it has gathered some positive momentum," said Ripken. "Maybe

"I THINK I'VE SHOWN I'M A GOOD PLAYER, AND I'VE ACCOMPLISHED OTHER THINGS IN MY CAREER BESIDES THE STREAK."

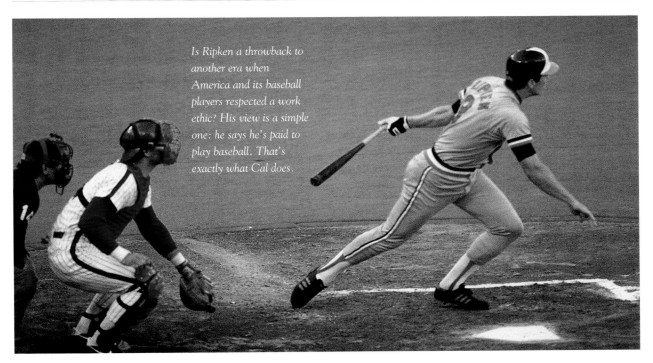

Is Ripken a throwback to another era when America and its baseball players respected a work ethic? His view is a simple one: he says he's paid to play baseball. That's exactly what Cal does.

that's the reason I've become a little more at peace in dealing with it, or accepting that it even exists. I think I fought it for years, because it wasn't my overall identity and it wasn't something I set out to do.

"Now, I think I've accepted that it's a part of what's going on. I still have to try to concentrate on doing what I do, and that's playing on a daily basis."

Ripken is a throwback to another era, when America and its baseball players respected a work ethic. As he likes to say, he's paid to play baseball every day, and that's what he does.

That's why he resents the attention, and why it is foreign to him to have to defend himself for playing through slumps.

The criticism peaked in 1990, when he hit a career-low .250, and struggled to hit 21 homers and 84 RBI. Since that was the year he passed Scott, it was

inevitable he would be asked if The Streak was hurting him, and if The Streak was his motivation for not taking a day off.

Ripken always bristled at those suggestions, and although he never said it was so, it seemed he used the

1991 season to silence his critics. Ripken won his second Most Valuable Player Award that year (his first was in 1983) with career-highs in average (.323), homers (34) and RBI

"I'M A BASEBALL PLAYER, AND MY FATHER TAUGHT ME THE IMPORTANCE OF BEING IN THE LINE-UP EVERY DAY AND HAVING YOUR TEAMMATES BE ABLE TO DEPEND ON YOU."

(114). For good measure, he was the MVP of the All-Star Game, hitting a three-run homer the day after winning the home run hitting contest with 12 in 22 swings.

Never again has he had to answer those questions, which may have removed his biggest obstacle of concentration.

"It's easier to deal with when you don't have to defend the position that you want to play," said Ripken, 35, a 13-time American League All-Star with two Gold Gloves.

"The most difficult part of the streak is when you're struggling and when you're not hitting well. It's frustrating enough not to hit well, and it's even more frustrating to defend your desire to be in the line-up, or to defend the reason you're in the line-up."

Ripken always defends himself by saying there are ways to help his team win

On August 24, 1992, Cal shook hands with Orioles General Manager Roland Hemond after signing his long-term contract with the club. Incidentally, the date also happened to be Cal's 32nd birthday. Nice present!

other than hitting — and that's why he was signed to a five-year, $30.5 million contract on August 24, 1992, his 32nd birthday.

"You never know what's going to happen in a game," said Ripken. "Maybe you start a double-play in the ninth inning that ends the game, or maybe you move a runner over in the third and he scores what proves to be the winning run, or maybe, because of your presence in the line-up, they pitch differently to other guys.

The Best Deserves the Best... In 1992, Baltimore's Oriole Park at Camden Yards quickly received accolades as many called it "the best ballpark in the country." It's only fitting that Cal Ripken calls it home.

"I always felt if the manager put my name in the line-up, he did it because he thought I was the best player at that position and could help the team win. That's why I'm there."

And, will always be there. Lou Gehrig would be proud.

What follows is a collection of stories which celebrate Cal's tremendous and history-making career — articles about Cal, his family, his colleagues, and his dedication to the game of baseball. Over and over, people are saying the same thing about Cal Ripken: that he is a professional through and through, and that his commitment to playing each day is remarkable.

Cal Ripken deserves the attention The Streak has bestowed him. ■

13

"I always felt that if the manager put my name in the line-up, he did it because he thought I was the best player at that position and could help the team win. That's why I'm there." — Cal Ripken

"I still want to focus on being a better player next season and in the future."

~ CAL RIPKEN JR ~

Chapter 2

Offensively Speaking

BY
GORDON BEARD

CAL RIPKEN CAN CERTAINLY look acrobatic and graceful while backhanding a grounder in the hole or making a 360-degree turn to throw out a batter after snaring a grounder up the middle.

That kind of talent has enabled Cal to hold outright or share 11 Major League or American League fielding records, including fewest errors (3) in a season, and has led to two Gold Glove awards.

But take it from Brooks Robinson, the legendary Orioles third baseman who copped a record 16 Gold Gloves for fielding excellence during his Hall of Fame career: that's not how you earn lucrative paychecks.

"I don't get paid for my fielding," Brooks used to say before he retired in 1977. And he reiterated the same thought recently while discussing Cal's glittering career.

"Even though times have changed," Brooks said, referring to the mega-buck salaries of the current players, "you still don't make the big money unless you can hit."

When young Cal reached the big leagues in 1981, Brooks said, "There was some doubt about his hitting. But as he grew bigger and stronger, he became better and better."

Cal hit only .128 (5 for 39) in 23 games with the O's at the end of the 1991 season, and he started 1982 in a 7 for 55 slump. At that point, his Major League average over two seasons was a puny .121 (12 for 99).

By the end of the season, however, he had upped his average to .264. With 28 home runs and 93 runs batted in, Cal edged Kent Hrbek of the Minnesota Twins to win American League Rookie of the Year honors.

Those numbers have pretty much become the norm for Cal over the years. He entered the 1995 season with a .277 career batting mark, while averaging 24 homers and 91 RBI for 13 seasons.

"I don't know why people insist on comparing Cal to other shortstops," said Frank Robinson, the Orioles assistant general manager. "Compared to slap hitters like (Mark) Belanger, sure he's going to be better. He compares favorably to anybody."

Over the last 13 years, Cal leads the Major Leagues in extra-base hits, with 764 entering this season. Through the same period, Cal was second to Eddie Murray with 1,179 runs batted in, and third to Murray and Andre Dawson with 310 homers.

He is one of only nine players ever to hit 20 or more home runs in their first 10 full seasons, joining the likes of Ted Williams, Rocky Colavito, Billy Williams, Joe

Cal's offensive numbers are impressive: he leads active players in extra-base hits with 764 going into the '95 season. He's also second to pal Eddie Murray with 1,179 RBI and 3rd to Murray and Andre Dawson in homers with 310.

16

RIPKEN IS ONE OF ONLY NINE PLAYERS TO EVER HIT 20 OR MORE HOME RUNS IN THEIR FIRST 10 FULL SEASONS.

DiMaggio, Willie Mays, Reggie Jackson, Eddie Mathews, and Frank Robinson himself. That list definitely doesn't include any slap hitters.

Cal's averages of 24 homers and 91 RBI a season compare favorably with those of Frank Robinson. The former Orioles outfielder and Hall of Famer averaged 30 homers and 94 RBI over 19 seasons before his numbers declined (while playing only part-time in his final two years in the Major Leagues).

Cal literally grew up in a baseball family, following his father Cal Sr. in his trek through the minor leagues before reaching the Orioles as a coach and, eventually, as the manager.

Cal grew up in baseball and quickly learned to respect the game and the work ethic. "I had a very good teacher in my dad," said Cal.

"I've been exposed to baseball for a long, long time," Cal said, "and I had a very good teacher in my dad. Being around major leaguers as I grew up made it easier for me to adjust when I came up (to the majors). A lot of guys are intimidated at first."

Former Kansas City pitcher Paul Splittorff, now a broadcaster for the Royals, expanded on that train of thought during a recent visit to Camden Yards. "Kids who grow up around the park know that players are human beings, just regular people," he said, "so it's a little easier early-on for them.

"He was a run producer from the day he got here, and a surprisingly good breaking-ball hitter. He had an idea of the strike zone and how the game was played."

"I think his father was more of a psychological plus for him than anything else," observed John Lowenstein, Junior's former teammate and now an Orioles broadcaster. "His dad's work ethic was just unbelievable and I think that's where Cal got his."

Lowenstein remembers that after Cal was named Rookie of the Year in 1982 and Most Valuable Player in 1983, Cal Sr. cautioned: "Don't judge Cal by what he does the first two or three years. Let him play 10 years and then start making judgments."

Well, that time period has expired and, despite rave notices that accompany

"You never get to a point where you know it all or can do it all," explains Ripken when talking about striving for perfection both offensively and defensively.

With a Little Help From My Friends

ONE OF LIFE'S *most certain lessons is that it helps to have friends in powerful places. Lou Gehrig enjoyed the kinship of quite a few powerful mates in his line-up with Murderers Row, or the Bronx Bombers, if you will. He played with Hall of Famers Babe Ruth, Bill Dickey and Earle Combs. Batting cleanup behind the "Bambino," he helped protect Ruth in the order.*

Cal had one team-mate of certain Hall of Fame caliber—Eddie Murray. Murray with his 3,000 hits and almost 500 homers has nothing for which to apologize. His career is remarkable.

To date Cal has played in only one World Series — 1983. Lou played in 1926, 1927, 1928, 1932, 1936, 1937, and 1938. ☐

Cal's fielding and hitting acumen and his assault on Lou Gehrig's consecutive game streak of 2,130, the Orioles shortstop is not content to rest on his laurels.

"You never get to the point where you know it all or can do it all," Cal said, explaining his never-ending strive for perfection on both offense and defense. "It's a game of constant adjustments. If you don't experiment and try things, you're going to 'wash out' pretty quickly."

To ease the way for his many accomplishments, Cal has a knack for lessening the daily tedium and blunting possible pressures. You might see him race Tim Bishop, the team's strength and conditioning coach, to the dugout after doing some pre-game stretching in the outfield.

It's not only Cal's consecutive game streak record that's amazing, but also his overall work ethic. Cal rarely misses infield or batting practice.

Or, when the team takes the field at the start of the game, you'll likely see Cal racing outfielder Brady Anderson to the second base bag on the way to their defensive positions. In the clubhouse, Cal will be the one promoting some form of roughhousing, which he usually wins because of his size.

"I'm always looking for some way to enjoy what we do, to figure out some kind of 'game within a game,'" he said. "If you make practice fun, if you make the game fun, I think that's helpful. If you do the same things over and over, the game itself can become pretty monotonous. You have to run out onto the field at least nine times a game, so you might as well make a sport of it."

Cal remembers his father saying how much he loved to come to the ballpark, that it made him happy just to put on his uniform.

"I never quite understood that," he said, "although I've always enjoyed coming to the park. But after the long off-season last year, and having baseball taken away for so long, I think I now can better understand my dad's enthusiasm."

Cal's typical low-key approach to his accomplishments has never varied. Most of the time, he's embarrassed by the attention given him and he's always looking ahead for new goals to reach.

In 1983, when he led the league with 211 hits, 47 doubles and 121 runs, and added 27 homers and 102 RBI on the way to the MVP award, Cal said: "I'm still hungry. I don't know if the numbers will be the same, but I'm going to try and improve."

The O's went 34-10 down the stretch to win the Eastern Division by six games. During that spurt, Cal hit .391 (75-192) with 14 doubles, 9 homers, 30 RBI, and 40 runs scored. He was named the American League's Player of the Month for September.

At the time, manager Joe Altobelli said, "We label guys too quickly in this game, but I call him a 'natural.' He's the kid who,

had he gone into football, would have caught the winning touchdown. If it were basketball, he would have scored the winning basket."

Asked recently for his reflections of Cal during his managerial days (1983-85), Altobelli recalled telling Cal, "We won't do this again next year," after he had played every inning of the 1983 season.

"But he did it again in 1984, and in 1985 right up until I left the club," Altobelli said, "and he still hasn't missed a game. I once asked Cal why he didn't want just a couple innings off and he said, 'When I first came up, I used to sit on the bench, then once I'd go in, I didn't want to come out again.'"

Cal played in 8,243 consecutive innings, believed to be the longest such streak in baseball history, before Cal Sr., then the manager, sat him down in the 8th inning of an 18-3 loss to the Toronto Blue Jays in 1987.

Junior was on base when the inning ended, and brother Bill instinctively grabbed Cal's glove on the dugout steps to take it to him on the field.

"That's the wrong glove," Cal Sr. said.

"No, this is Cal's," said Bill.

"Ron Washington's going in."

Just like that, the streak ended. No fuss, no argument. Cal took it just like a Ripken should.

"It was an eerie feeling, a weird feeling," Cal said. "My first thought was 'OK.' What else could I say? The manager has his say in the way the club is run. I'm a player. I do what the manager tells me."

In 1991, Cal won another MVP award, and was the only player in the American League to finish in the Top Ten in hits (210), homers (34), average (.323) and RBI (114). He became only the 10th player in league history to hit

In 1991 at Toronto's SkyDome, Cal became the 4th Oriole to win the All-Star Most Valuable Player Award. The other Orioles to receive All-Star MVP Awards were: Billy O'Dell in 1958; Brooks Robinson in 1966; and Frank Robinson in 1971.

Cal also received the MVP Award that year, becoming the only player in AL history to win the award on a sub .500 team.

ALTOBELLI ONCE ASKED CAL WHY HE DIDN'T WANT TO TAKE A COUPLE OF INNINGS OFF AND HE SAID, "WHEN I FIRST CAME UP, I USED TO SIT ON THE BENCH, THEN ONCE I'D GO IN, I DIDN'T WANT TO COME OUT AGAIN."

more than 30 homers and strike out less than 50 times (46) in a season.

Cal also led the majors with 85 extra-base hits, 368 total bases, and 73 multi-hit games, and was second with 210 hits and 46 doubles. He again finished strongly in September, as he did in 1983, and was named the AL Player of the Month with a .349 average, eight home runs and 27 RBI.

But there was no complacency. "I still want to focus on being a better player next season and in the future," he said.

After a mini-slump in August, Cal did the unthinkable and skipped batting practice for about a week in September, while studiously avoiding Cal Sr.

"I come from a family that preaches practice," he said, while explaining how he hid out among the pitchers shagging fly balls. "I knew that if I talked with my dad, he would tell me that I was going to hurt myself by not taking BP, so I tried not to talk with him very much."

The Iron Man continues to strive to better himself as an offensive player. Whether it's working on his swing, adjusting his stance, or altering his mental approach, he's been successful at trying new tactics.

Cal also was named the MVP of the All-Star game in 1991, when he had a single and a three-run homer in the American League's 4-2 victory. In the home-run hitting contest the day before the game, Cal hit 12 homers out of Toronto's SkyDome in just 22 swings.

It was truly an incredible year for Cal, but he was uncomfortable about being called one of the game's best.

After learning he had won the award, Cal said, "I didn't think that I would be this excited. I tried to downplay it. I was very pleased with my season, but I didn't think it would come to this."

But even while celebrating, Cal was mindful of his public image. Before a news conference at Camden Yards, he said on television that he was celebrating the award by drinking champagne in his kitchen.

Later, at the news conference, he drank a toast in a champagne glass...filled with milk. "This will help restore my image," he said.

Cal's average had slipped to .257 in 1989 and to .250 in 1990, and Cal thought that his days as a player might be numbered. He spent the winter of 1990 working on a new approach at the plate, saw results in spring training, and was consistent throughout the 1991 season.

Cal conferred with manager Frank Robinson, hitting coach Tom McCraw, and his father to relocate theories he had abandoned. "I spread out more at the plate," he said, "put some flex in my knees and let the ball come to me rather than searching for it. I used my hands more in the swing."

Cal also downplayed a couple of other milestones in his career, like when he became the all-time home run leader among shortstops and when he reached the 2,000-hit plateau.

A home run on July 15, 1993, his 278th as a shortstop, moved Cal past Hall of Famer Ernie Banks. But because of a mix-up in the record-keeping, the mark wasn't discovered until after the season and it was finally recognized at Camden Yards on February 9, 1994.

Banks had been credited with 16 homers as a shortstop when he was actually playing first base at the time, reducing his mark as a shortstop to 277. The Orioles had been told four years earlier, when they started to track Ripken's homers, that Banks had hit 293.

"I'm very honored to be mentioned with the likes of Mr. Ernie Banks," Cal said at the ceremony attended by Banks. "In a list of achievements, I'm not sure where this ranks. For me, team play and accomplishments like playing in a World Series are what's important."

After getting his 2,000th hit, Cal said, "I don't know what this means necessarily, except that you have to be around a long time to do it. I'm more concerned about being more consistent this season."

Cal's even a bit uneasy about the publicity surrounding his amazing consecutive game streak, saying he was singled out "just for showing up."

Meeting with the media in California, as he has in each city on the road, Cal talked about being criticized for continuing to play while slumping at the plate: "It was so foreign to me to have to defend my desire to play that I tended to fight

In 1993, Ripken hit a home run ball to left field near the bullpens in Oriole Park. The home run didn't receive any noteworthy recognition until early in 1994 when it was discovered that it was Cal's 278th, moving him past Ernie Banks in most home runs by a shortstop.

A press conference was held at Oriole Park for Ripken on February 9 that year commemorating the achievement. Ernie Banks flew in for the event.

The seat in left field is now painted orange, marking the momentous home run.

it and let it bother me. It was as if the problem would be magically fixed if I came out of the line-up, but I always felt that would be running away from the problem. I was taught by my dad to figure out what was going on and fix it."

In trying to fix such problems, Cal sometimes works on his stance in the batter's box. "I've never seen more drastic changes," said Frank Robinson, "not the subtle changes that most guys make. But you have to work them out for yourself, and Cal does what's comfortable and successful for him."

"The striving for perfection is not unusual among the game's better players," said Orioles coach Elrod Hendricks. "They always want to be better, they're never satisfied with yesterday's old news. They look forward to today and tomorrow to become a little better."

Whatever else the critics say about Cal, they always come back to the basics...he's a student of the game, a team player, and a genuine pro's pro. Orioles coach Al Bumbry said of his former teammate, "He believes in playing the complete game and he has the same routine every day...the hitting, fielding, exercising and stretching, no matter what his frame of mind. That's why he's been so consistent and why he's respected by his peers."

"My biggest goal," Cal said, "is that when my career is over and I'm sitting in a rocking chair, I don't have any regrets. I want to feel satisfied that I played as long as I could and did as well as I could do. When it's over, I want to be able to say I did all I could do...that there was no more." ■

Critics agree about Cal as an offensive player—He is a student of the game, a team player, and a genuine pro's pro. He seems to be able to master his techniques with practice. "I was always taught by my dad to figure out what was going on and fix it."

"His glove,
not his bat, has
always been his
greatest weapon."

~ TOM BOSWELL ~

Chapter 3

Ripken: For the Defense

BY BOB BROWN

BEFORE HE PUTS HIS glove and bat away, Cal Ripken Jr. will hold most of the Orioles' career batting records: most this, most that, most just about everything. The best lifetime batting average will escape him. So will triples and stolen bases, but not much else.

To be sure, he's made enormous contributions to the Orioles' offensive production over the past 14 seasons.

And yet, as good as he's been with his bat, he's been even better with his glove...and his arm.

Forget about all those critics who say, "He's too tall, he's too big, he's too slow to play shortstop." Sure, and Babe Ruth was too fat to be the game's greatest slugger.

At 6'4", he's the tallest regular shortstop ever; at 225, he could also be the heaviest. But he's probably also the smartest, most intuitive, and most diligent ever to have played that position.

Since early in 1982, he has been the most durable player at his or any other position that baseball has ever known. And for the past seven years, he's been the most consistent

fielding shortstop in history.

This is not to say that he has the greatest range among shortstops. Others, past and present (most notably the legendary Ozzie Smith), can lay claim to that title. But Cal compensates with instinct and knowledge, by knowing the hitters' tendencies, and shading them according to the pitcher, the kind of pitch to be thrown and its location. It's called "cheating," but it's perfectly legal, and though he'll occasionally get burned by leaning the wrong way, it won't happen often.

And lest we forget, his right arm ranks at the top of any scale in both strength and accuracy.

Cal is not the most acrobatic or crowd-pleasing shortstop you've ever seen. He's never done any of Ozzie Smith's patented flips (if he had, chances are Lou Gehrig's endurance record would have survived forever). You might say his defensive style is dull, unless you're a true baseball fan who recognizes the difficulty of what he does afield, game after game, season after season.

Brooks Robinson used to delight us with his diving stops, then pick himself up and throw the batter out. You can do that at third (though no one has ever

Ripken is the tallest ever to play shortstop regularly in the majors. Other 6'4" major leaguers who have played some shortstop include Ray Busse (Houston, '71-'74) and former Orioles Enos Cabell and Jamie Quirk.

Cal has played in more games than any other shortstop in Orioles history, surpassing Mark Belanger, who held the record with 1,898. Only Brooks Robinson has played more games at one position in club history with 2,870 at third base.

done it quite as consistently as Brooks), but not so often at short, where you're farther away from first base and have less time to get off the throw.

As Brooks says about Cal, "You don't see him on the highlight shows, making all those flashy plays. To appreciate a guy like Cal, you have to see him every day. The way he positions himself, the strong arm, everything he does."

Cal concurs. "If people watch me for only a few games, nothing stands out. If they watch over a season, maybe they have a different opinion."

But there was a play, not so long ago (July 6, '95 in Chicago), when his diving catch of a Lance Johnson line drive, which was headed for center field with two out and the tying run on second in the eighth inning, won a game for the Orioles.

Cal has had his share of batting slumps over the years. And there have been times when somebody else might have provided more offense in the line-up. But in a game in which pitching and defense are so critical, there has never been a man on the Orioles bench during the past 14 seasons who has been — you should pardon the expression — in the same ballpark with Cal Ripken as a shortstop.

The considerable controversy that attended Cal's conversion from third to short is all but forgotten now. It happened in 1982 when Earl Weaver dictated

the switch, and it wasn't a popular move. Cal had played short off and on in the minors, but when Earl wrote his name into the line-up on July 1 and put the number "6" after it, the "too big, too slow" howls echoed everywhere.

It is a popular notion that the Orioles haven't been adequately staffed at third base since Brooks stepped down as an everyday player. But that isn't true. Doug DeCinces wasn't Brooks' equal at that position, but he was far more than adequate, and still ranks as the second best hot-corner custodian in club history.

When DeCinces was traded to the Angels, Cal took over and, had he remained there, chances are that Baltimore, by now, could lay claim to the two best fielding third basemen of all time.

But Weaver had a big problem at short. Mark Belanger's heir apparent was a prospect named Bob Bonner, a good-field, no-hit type who never reached his potential, some say, because he didn't respond well to Earl's blunt managerial style. Lenn Sakata, the other candidate, was a utility player not equipped to handle the job on an everyday basis.

So, Weaver made the move. He told Cal, "I just want you to catch the ball, take your time and make a good throw. If he's out, he's out. If he's safe, he's only on first base."

And though the transfer created a void at third that has been filled only sporadically since then, putting Cal Ripken at shortstop solved a bigger dilemma at a more difficult position for 14 years...and counting. ≈

Cal has won only two Gold Gloves during his career (1991 and 1992). Why? Perhaps, because the managers and coaches, who vote in the annual election for the best defensive players at each position,

The highest fielding percentage in one season by a major league shortstop went to Cal Ripken in 1990. He set a major league record with a .996 fielding percentage with 242 putouts, 435 assists, 680 total chances, and only three errors.

The Tale of Two Shortstops

THE OVERWHELMING CONSENSUS *is that the Cardinals' Ozzie Smith is the greatest defensive shortstop of this or any other era. That's a difficult point to argue. Smith has led his league in each of the following categories a cumulative 28 times during his 17 years in the National League (beginning 1978): assists (8), putouts (2), chances per game (5), double plays (5) and percentage (8).*

But the man who describes himself as "big and slow and cumbersome in a lot of ways," compared to shortstops like Luis Aparicio, Belanger and Smith, has led the American League in assists (7), putouts (6), chances per game (3), double plays (7) and percentage (3) a total of 26 times in 13 seasons.

The Washington Post's Tom Boswell researched that statistical comparison for a 1994 column in which he concluded:

"Ripken is the second-best defensive shortstop of his era. His glove, not his bat, has always been his greatest weapon.

"That such an historically adept and innovative fielder should also have more extra-base hits than any other player during his time in the majors (ed note: and more home runs than any shortstop ever) makes him ridiculously unique and valuable."

	Assists	Putouts	Chances per game	Double plays	Percentage
Ozzie Smith	8 years - led NL	2	5	5	8
Cal Ripken Jr.	7 years - led AL	6	3	7	3

A Case For the Record Books

HERE IS A LIST OF CAL'S *quantifiable accomplishments as a shortstop through the years:*

Fielding Records:
Highest fielding percentage, season
> **.996 (1990)** -ML

Fewest errors, season, 150 or more games
> **3 (1990)** -ML

Most consecutive errorless games, one or more seasons
> **95 (1990)** -ML

Most consecutive errorless chances, one or more seasons
> **431 (1990)** -ML

Most years led league in games
> **10 ('83-'84, '87-'94)*** -ML

Most consecutive games played, one position
> **continuing** -ML

Most years leading league in double plays
> **7 ('83-'85, '89, '91-'92, '94)** -ML

Most years leading league in putouts (tied)
> **6 ('84-'85, '88-'89, '91-'92)** -ML

Most assists, season
> **583 (1984)** -AL

ML-Major League; AL-American League

*-though he played every Orioles game in '85-'86, Tony Fernandez did, too, and the Blue Jays played one more game than the Orioles in each of those years.

Other Fielding Distinctions
Fielding Percentage: *Through last season, Cal ranked fourth (.97837) on the all-time major league list in highest career fielding percentage, behind Larry Bowa (.97968), Tony Fernandez (.97965), and Ozzie Smith (.97863). However, over the past six seasons (beginning 1989), Cal's percentage has been .9863.*

Errors per Chance: *Cal and Ozzie have averaged one error every 47 chances during their major league careers. During the last six seasons, Cal has committed only one error every 73 chances. For comparison's sake, while he was winning eight Gold Gloves at shortstop for the Orioles, Mark Belanger erred on an average of once in 43 chances, and the league average in 1994 by shortstops was one error every 33 chances.*

Games Played: *By the time he surpasses Lou Gehrig's record, on or about September 6, he will have appeared in 2,119 games at shortstop, third on the American League list behind Aparicio (2,581) and Luke Appling (2,218).*

Double Plays: *Despite playing with at least 29 different keystone partners in an often turbulent period for the Orioles, Cal will have moved up to third on the all-time major league list, behind Aparicio and Smith, by the end of this season.*

still think, stereotypically, that the best shortstops have to be sleek and speedy.

Whether they know it or not, Cal Ripken has changed all that.

≈

It hasn't been an easy ride for Cal Ripken during his record-setting years as the Orioles shortstop. His brother, Bill, who might have been his best defensive partner at second base, was let go.

His father was dismissed as manager six games into the worst season the Orioles have ever experienced (1988), and several years later was demoted from the coaching staff.

And since 1983 when he earned his first MVP award, his beloved Orioles have seriously contended for a division title only once (1989).

"When I first came up to the big leagues, I was spoiled rotten," he remarked several years ago. "A bad year for the Orioles was winning 90 games and finishing second. We won 94 games my first year, the World Series my second year. I figured, well, this is the way it's supposed to be."

30

During the consecutive games streak, Cal has been replaced at short by 9 players 56 times.

The replacements include:

Tim Hulett, 22
Juan Bell, 12
Rene Gonzalez, 9
Manny Alexander, 5
Marty Brown, 3
Jeff McKnight, 2
Ron Washington, 1
Pete Stanicek, 1
Steve Scarsone, 1

BUT IN THE END, JUST AS IN THE CASES OF HALL OF FAMERS LUIS APARICIO AND BROOKS ROBINSON, IT WILL BE HIS DAY-TO-DAY FIELDING BRILLIANCE OVER THE LONG HAUL AT THE DIAMOND'S MOST CHALLENGING POSITION THAT ASSURES HIS FIRST-BALLOT ELECTION.

Cal has won two Gold Glove Awards—one in 1991 and one in 1992. He is the only Oriole to win a Gold Glove award in the past 10 years.

Cal has also averaged only one error for every 47 chances. Mark Belanger had the previous best by an Orioles shortstop—one every 43 chances.

Through it all, he has remained the consummate professional. He changed positions in the middle of a season, learned to play that position by working harder than his peers and using his superior intelligence and instincts to make up for his size and lack of foot speed, suffered through the inevitable batting slumps without letting them affect the quality of his fielding; weathered the intense, incessant pressure of chasing an "unbreakable" record; and never lost his commitment to winning or to his team over more than a decade of disappointment.

By the time he retires, Cal Ripken's cumulative offensive credentials, along with his incredible eclipse of Lou Gehrig's monument to durability, will offer substantial support to his candidacy for the Baseball Hall of Fame.

But in the end, just as in the cases of Hall of Famers Luis Aparicio and Brooks Robinson, it will be his day-to-day fielding brilliance over the long haul at the diamond's most challenging position that assures his first-ballot election. ■

"If it's anything
we share, it's desire,
stubbornness, and a
love of the game."

~ Cal Ripken Jr ~

Chapter 4

Baseball's Iron Age

BY
MIKE GESKER

Historians date the "Iron Age" from the time iron metallurgy was invented in Europe some time around 1,000 B.C. Fortunately for all of us this was accomplished roughly 30 centuries before the introduction of Euro-Disney into France. Otherwise, most Western Civilization classes would commence with the Eisner Age. For those of you who skipped school the day these facts were first broached, the "Iron Age" succeeded the Stone and Bronze Ages, and marked the use of tools and weapons made of iron. It was also during this period that the first "ironware" party was held by an obnoxious neighbor pushing spears and daggers in a grand pyramid scheme.

Well, fans, we're right, smack-dab in the middle of another amazing period. Future historians may very well consider the 20th century the sequel to the "Iron Age." We are witnessing the second of two remarkably gifted students of baseball, who give new meaning to the term "Perfect Attendance." Calvin Edwin Ripken Jr. is following a course charted by only one other North American baseball player. (The geographic distinction is necessary because Sachio Kinugasa played in 2,215 consecutive games for the Hiroshima Carp

WE'RE HERE TO HONOR A PAIR OF PLAYERS WHOSE MAGNIFICENT ACCOMPLISHMENTS ON THE FIELD SIMPLY DEFINE THE GAME.

from October 19, 1970 through October 22, 1987.) Before you get too excited and reach for the cellular phone, at no time during this treatise will we be conducting any insta-polls or telephone surveys, ala local news programs, to see whom you think is the better player: Cal, the "Iron Man," or Henry Louis Gehrig, the "Iron Horse." This is not a ratings period or "Sweeps Week." We're here to honor a pair of players whose magnificent accomplishments on the field simply define the game itself. Neither Cal nor Lou deserves to be remembered solely for the footprints they leave in the shifting statistical sands of the National Pastime.

Ripken is scheduled to break the 2,130 consecutive game streak held by Mr. Gehrig on Wednesday, September 6, against the California Angels at Oriole Park at Camden Yards. The ballpark holds 48,262 people. Two million fans will claim they were there.

Cal's streak began quietly on May 30, 1982. Oriole Manager Earl Weaver penciled Ripken's name in at third base. You could have bet Fort McHenry, the Shot Tower and the Block that Cal was destined to play his career on "the hot-corner." Brooks Robinson ended his sto-

Stranger Than Fiction

YOU DON'T HAVE to be Nostradamus or Oliver Stone to understand there are pretty powerful forces at work that destined Cal to be the one to break Lou's record.

Just look at the numbers. Lou and Cal both have nine letters in their names. There are nine men on a baseball team.

Lou wore number 4; Cal wears the number 8. Eight is a multiple of four.

Lou played first base, or the number three position, if you're scoring. Cal is a shortstop, or the number 6 position. A multiple of three. Exactly twice the number, the same as the uniform numerals. Lou played on the right side of the infield, but threw and batted left-handed. Cal, on the other hand, plays on the left side of the infield, but bats and throws right-handed.

It really gets too eerie from here on. Lou played for the New York Yankees. The Yankees used to be the Baltimore Orioles in 1901 and 1902. And Cal plays for the very same Baltimore Orioles. Gehrig played alongside Babe Ruth. Cal plays in the Bambino's hometown.

Cal: A Portrait of Concentration and Perfect Positioning.

rybook career and retired after the 1977 season. Heir apparent Doug DeCinces and pitcher Jeff Schneider were traded to the California Angels for "Disco" Dan Ford on January 28, 1982.

Cal seemed the perfect fit. Anyone who knows anything about baseball knows you don't put 6'4", 220-pound, slugging stars at shortstop. For years, many Baltimoreans thought there was a section in the rulebook that prohibited shortstops from weighing more than 150 pounds. Little Luis Aparicio and Mark Belanger were built like greyhounds with gloves.

The day before, on May 29, Floyd "Sugar Bear" Rayford played third in the second half of a double-header against the Toronto Blue Jays. The rest, as they say, is history. Cal remained the regular third baseman for the next month. But he was only a fleeting tenant. On July 1, 1982, he finally built his home at shortstop.

During Cal's incredible run, 3,700 major leaguers have gone on the disabled list. The other 27 major league clubs have used a total of 522 shortstops in the meantime.

It's hard to imagine now how controversial the move of Cal to short by Earl Weaver was at the time. That topic alone kept local radio talk shows on the air with hundreds of irate callers, sprinkled liberally among the phoners who were abducted by aliens flying space vehicles shaped like the AMC Pacer. The saint-

Life in the trenches around second base is routinely interrupted by the violent rush of baserunner's bayonets — the groin-high thrust of flying spikes. Just one of the many occupational hazards Cal has endured during his streak.

ed "Earl of Baltimore" was declared a heretic, and another Inquisition was in the making. The move was as blasphemous as suggesting that Mother Theresa go out for a few brewskies.

Well, it took some of us a little longer than others to realize that Earl always knew something we didn't. That strategic move alone should be good enough to send Weaver to the Hall of Fame.

Surprisingly, the Birds' won-loss record during Cal's amazing run is not quite .500 baseball (not a bad batting average, but a less than stellar winning percentage). This is certainly not an indictment of Cal's abilities, merely ample

TRY TURNING A DOUBLE-PLAY ABOUT 200 TIMES A SEASON AND SEE WHAT KIND OF INSURANCE YOU CAN PICK UP. WELL, THAT CRAZY STUNT IS THE VERY ESSENCE OF THE SHORTSTOP POSITION.

evidence that his very respectable offensive stats could only improve with better teammates. The 1988 Orioles were the very antithesis of the 1927 Yankees. During the 13+ seasons of the streak, Cal has stung more extra base hits than any other player in the game, with over 800. His nearest competitors are Andre Dawson, with 741, and Cal's former mentor Eddie Murray, with 742.

Earl Weaver: The Baltimore Orioles answer to Horace Greeley proclaimed, "Go to short, young man. Go to short!"

Ever try to tie your shoelaces while in a revolving door? How about attempting to pick up a dime off the street in the middle of rush hour traffic? Run with the bulls? Or worse yet, make an effort to step on a rectangular bag milliseconds before Frank Thomas, Don Baylor, or Dave Winfield wanted to occupy the same space? You don't have to be a genius to understand the basic physics at work here. Something's gotta give.

Lou Gehrig and Babe Ruth literally defined the roles of the number 3 and 4 hitters. In 1929, the Yankees wore numbers on their uniforms for the first time. Their awesome batting order determined the numerals.

Try turning a double-play about 200 times a season and see what kind of insurance you can pick up. Well, that crazy stunt is the very essence of the shortstop position. Players with nicknames like "Pee Wee," "The Scooter," "The Blade," and "The Wizard of Oz," seemed to float like hummingbirds high above the melee at second base. With Cal's less than gossamer-like

A Curmudgeon's Perspective

IF YOU'RE IN LOVE with artificial turf, the designated hitter, or the modern Field Marshall Erwin Rommel Desert Fox sunglasses worn today in the field, and at bat, for Pete's sake!, this section is not for you. This section is for those stout-hearted souls who firmly believe Indians' third baseman Jim Thome should be inducted immediately into Cooperstown because he wears his socks and pants the way they're supposed to be worn.

And it goes without saying that any cap that is mesh and/or with an adjustable headband is not a "real" baseball hat.

Know why the modern game isn't as good? Batting gloves.

No hitter ever averaged over .400, drove in 190 runs in a season, or hit 60 or more homers a year wearing batting gloves. What's the problem? Fear of splinters? Dutch Elm Disease? Allergic to pine tar? You don't have to ride the pine to feel the wood.

The first night baseball game was played May 25, 1935 at Crosley Field in Cincinnati. That means Lou Gehrig played virtually his whole career under the sun. Is it easier to see the ball in daylight? The batters who tried to pick up the spin on the ball coming out of the white houses beyond the fences of Memorial Stadium would readily disagree.

Which brings us to the uniforms. Until the advent of double-knit fabrics in the early '70s, ballplayers went to work in wool flannel, or wool and cotton blends. Surprisingly enough, the first half-century of baseball wasn't played during the ice age. Summer in St. Louis could boast the same heat and humidity as Baltimore today. They played ball under the blistering sun in those uniforms with longer sleeves, and they frequently had two games the same day. Heavy, water-soaked jerseys robbed precious split seconds in the swing of a bat, or sprint to a base. Unbelievable. The weight of the flannels was not reduced much until after the Second World War — well after Lou left the game.

Gehrig and his contemporaries' mitts were only slightly larger than a hotdog bun. Today, Boston's Mike Greenwell has a glove big enough to apply for statehood. Naturally, more base hits fell when the game was younger.

So, you can see the differences in the players of yesteryear and those of today. It's in the batting gloves, the uniforms, and the mitts.

Let's bring back the costumes of the past—for old-time's sake.

Perhaps that's why "Turn Back the Clock" Day is always such a popular day.

Milk Money

WITH A SHREWD *agent and the right image, a talented athlete can muster a comfortable fortune from endorsements. Thanks to Michael and Shaq the National Basketball Association is the Fort Knox of sports.*

It seems Cal has been associated with milk longer than the U.S.D.A. He knocked Elsie the Cow out of the box long ago as the most recognized dairy spokesman. Milk and Cal spell a rich wholesomeness that is right out of a Norman Rockwell painting.

Lou, on the other hand, was associated with the very bane of the American Cancer Society's existence — tobacco. His smiling countenance appears in the corner of an ad for Camels. "'They Don't Get Your Wind,' Athletes say." reads the campaign. "So mild, athletes smoke as many as they please—and that's real mildness! So mild you can smoke all you want!" Holy lung cancer!

You can also see Lou enjoying the joys of Camels on the sheet music for a song his friend Fred Fisher wrote in 1935, "I Can't Get to First Base With You." ▫

physique, he doesn't accumulate many frequent flyer miles hovering around the bag. But somehow, Cal has not only managed to survive, he has thrived, as if he were Marshall Matt Dillon throwing rowdies out of the saloon for not saying "please" and "thank you" to Miss Kitty.

Typically Cal avoids comparing himself to Lou as a player. He obviously respects and admires "The Pride of the Yankees." A cursory look at the offensive statistics of both players bears him out. But there are great similarities in the way each approached the game as a profession. As Cal prepared to appear in his 13th All-Star Game he summed up his feeling about their distant relationship: "If it's anything we share, it's desire, stubbornness and a love of the game."

Of course, Lou Gehrig didn't have the chance to play in 13 All-Star Games because the "Mid-Summer Classic" wasn't inaugurated until 1933. Perhaps Lou's

Paul Krichell, the Yankee scout who signed Gehrig, also tried to woo Hank Greenberg to the Bronx. Greenberg extended his regrets and respect: "I'd never seen such brute strength. 'No way I'm going to sign with this team,' I said to myself. Not with him (Lou) playing first base."

most famous, or infamous, All-Star feat was being a part of "King" Carl Hubbell's devastating neutering of the American League's vaunted line-up in the 1934 game. "Meal Ticket" Hubbell and his well-mastered screwball fanned, in a row, Babe Ruth, Lou Gehrig, Jimmie Foxx, Al Simmons and Joe Cronin.

Obviously baseball has gone through some changes between 1939, the year Lou retired, and 1982, the year Cal's streak started. Not too many drastic changes.

Here are some of the most significant factors that affected the two eras: Pitching, especially relief pitching.

Yes, Lou Gehrig did have to face the Washington Senators' Fred Marberry. Now, to give you some idea of Mr. Marberry's demeanor on the mound, you only have to know that teammates dubbed him "Firpo" because of his striking resem-

"Lou was the most valuable player the Yankees ever had because he was a prime source of their greatest asset — an implied confidence in themselves and in every man on the club. Lou's pride as a big leaguer rubbed off on everyone who played with him."
— Stanley Frank

Other Differences Between the Era of the Double-header Versus the Age of the Wave

RADIO
Lou's Era
~ *The Lone Ranger*
~ *Fibber McGee and Molly*
~ *Fireside Chats*
Cal's Era
~ *Howard Stern*
~ *Rush Limbaugh*
~ *G. Gordon Liddy*

More evidence that civilization is rapidly hurdling toward the basement.

MUSICAL ROYALTY ON THE RADIO
Lou's Era
~ *Benny Goodman - "The King of Swing"*
Cal's Era
~ *"The Artist Formerly Known as Prince"*

THE MOVIES OF 1939
The Year Lou Gehrig Retired
~ *The Wizard of Oz*
~ *Goodbye Mr. Chips*
~ *Of Mice and Men*
~ *Gone With the Wind*
Not a bad line-up from top to bottom.
Cal's going to need more than Home Alone 5, Die Hard 6, and Under Siege 7 to beat that bunch. ▫

The Iron Man met the Iron Horse in Monument Park at Yankee Stadium. Sometimes photos speak louder than words.

blance to the Argentine heavyweight Luis Firpo, "the Wild Bull of the Pampas." Mr. Firpo deposited Jack Dempsey into the ringside seats during a heavyweight boxing match in 1923.

But the bullpen didn't really become a major factor in baseball until after World War II, when Hugh Casey of the Brooklyn Dodgers and Joe Page of the New York Yankees started to beat a path to the mound in the late 1940s.

It's only been in the last two decades that managers have turned their bullpens into deadly arsenals. Although Lou had to bat against "Firpo" he never had to step into the box during the late innings of a game and stare out at the likes of "the Eck," "Goose," "Sparky," "Tug," "the Wild Thing," or "The Mad Hungarian." Loosely translated, that's Dennis Eckersley, Richard Gossage, Albert Lyle, Frank McGraw, Mitchell Williams, and Alan Hrabosky.

So the players of Lou's era definitely had an advantage. Well, not so fast. While Murderers' Row didn't have to hit against those formidable forces, simple math indicates some of their disadvantages. Gehrig's Yankees were part of the American League with only eight teams. Naturally only seven of them were opponents. For the sake of argument we'll say each of the other teams had 10 pitchers on their roster. That meant that Lou and his mates saw 70 of the best pitchers in the game.

Today's Orioles are part of a 14-team league, with 13 opposing teams. Do the multiplication and you have 130 pitchers, almost twice as many. Has the talent pool doubled over the span of years?

The Iron Horse in what has become one of his most memorable photographs.

However, the players of Lou's time also didn't have Gatorade or Powerade, Sportscreme, or the high-tech training and rehabilitation facilities available today. No batting gloves, no batting helmets, but they did have one thing most of today's players don't — off-season jobs. They worked on farms, in factories, down in coal mines, sold insurance and cars. Fingers, toes, limbs, eyes or worse could be lost while making a living during the winter.

We can only hope that time, research, and common sense would have shown Lou the folly of his ways. But he also endorsed another product he actually used, "Ken-Wel Brand" baseball gloves — "The Glove Big Leaguers Use." Price: $10.00 each.

"To Lou Gehrig
We've been to the wars together;
We took our foes as they came;
And always you were the leader,
And ever you played the game.
Idol of cheering millions;
Records are yours by sheaves,
Iron of frame they hailed you,
Decked you with laurel leaves.
But higher than that we hold you,
We who have known you best;
Knowing the way you came through
Every human test.
Let this be a silent token
Of lasting friendship's gleam
And all that we've left unspoken
— Your pals of the Yankee team"
from a plaque presented to Lou.

A board game, made by the Rich Illinois Manufacturing Company of Morrison, Illinois, called "Lou Gehrig's Official Playball Board Game," no doubt on the Christmas list of thousands of young Larrupin' Lou fans.

Devotees could also sign up to be a member of "Lou Gehrig's Knot Hole League of America." Members received a blue and white patch to wear on their jacket, free passes to baseball games and an honorary Yankee contract.

Although Cal has made TV commercials for Adventure World and milk, and endorses Coca-Cola, he has yet to make the Hollywood connection. It may be a very fortunate circumstance for Cal. Lou's agent Christy Walsh apparently wasn't very discriminating. He encouraged Lou to pose in some publicity stills that might embarrass Madonna. Several shots have "The Iron Horse" wrapped in a spotted leopard outfit that should only be seen on a fraternity house sofa. Walsh saw Lou as the next Tarzan. Johnny Weissmuller never lost Jane and Cheetah to Gehrig, but Lou did find himself in a ten gallon hat, chaps and spurs in a movie called "Rawhide." He got equal billing in the 1938 20th Century Fox release with Smith Ballew. "The slugging star of the New York Yankees teams up with singin', scrappin' Smith Ballew...to give you your greatest action western," read one of the 60-minute long film's marquee cards.

Gehrig and some early replacement players. Lou and the Marx Brothers hailed from the same Yorkville neighborhood in New York City. Groucho, Lou, Chico, and Harpo — not a bad infield.

WHO WAS THE BETTER COMPOSER, BEETHOVEN OR MOZART? DON'T WASTE YOUR TIME. IT DOESN'T REALLY MATTER, DOES IT? WE REAP THE BOUNTY OF THEIR TALENTS, STRENGTHS, GENIUS, AND PERSPIRATION WITHOUT CAUSE OR MUCH INCLINATION TO COMPARE THEM.

The thousands of tempest-tossed immigrants who found a new life on New York's Ellis Island and beyond were sometimes issued a handy guide that strongly suggested that newcomers "Do not take a moment's rest. Run, do, work, and keep your own good in mind." Yorkville was just a few home run clouts away from the Statue of Liberty, and among the families that settled there were the Gehrigs, Cagneys and Marxs. America is a little better place today because Lou, Jimmy, Groucho, Chico and Harpo all followed that advice.

Mr. Timex.
Cal takes a licking and
keeps on ticking.

Who was the better composer, Beethoven or Mozart? The more important inventor, daVinci or Edison? Gifted painter, Michelangelo or Monet? Don't waste your time. It doesn't really matter, does it? We reap the bounty of their talents, strengths, genius, and perspiration without cause or much inclination to compare them. Likewise, Calvin Edwin Ripken and Henry Louis Gehrig should be admired together for their gritty devotion to the work ethic and absolutely splendid and quiet way they performed their chores on the diamond. Celebrate them. Don't compare them. Pick up a copy of *Total Baseball*. Skim the thousands of names. These two magnificent gentlemen stand alone...together.

"Pride of the Yankees," "Pride of the Orioles." Heck, they're the "Pride of the Country." We as a nation could use a little more "Iron" in our diet. ∎

"Cal has made it very clear to me that family is first, family's number one."

~ Kelly Ripken ~

Chapter 5

All in the Family

BY
JACK GILDEN

Other towns may reverently worship famous names like Maris and Mantle or Rose and Bench, but in any watering hole from Highlandtown to Hampden you can simply say Brooks, Frank or Boog, Brady or Cal. That's more than enough to fetch you knowing nods from the regulars and some snappy repartee from the stool next door. (Example: "I remember a game in '67. No, wait a minute, maybe it was '66. Anyway the point was…I was drivin' back from Eldersburg — that's where my people are — and I got the game on the rat-ee-oh and Boog's already mashed one. Then Frank slaps a tweener and he's settin' on second when here comes Brooksie…).

This is more than mere familiarity; it is something of the familial. In Baltimore, the cradle of Ruth and Kaline, ballplayers are part of the family.

But Cal Ripken Jr. is different. Baltimoreans haven't so much adopted him as they've been adopted by him. He has taken the town into his family.

In fact, for many years, invoking the name "Cal" didn't even refer to the famous shortstop. Once upon a time it stood for a rough-hewn, leather-faced cuss named Cal Ripken Sr. Vaguely reminiscent of the team's genius manager, Earl Weaver, Cal Sr. was a former minor-league catcher who played an enormously important role in making the Orioles farm system one of the finest in the game.

For 14 summers he toiled in the remotest villages of this vast republic — underneath searing Southern suns; on windswept heartland prairies; in lonely upstate towns; and even on the soaking wet sod of the Pacific Northwest.

Wherever there was a ball game and a few crackers or cowboys to watch it, Cal Sr. was there teaching unpolished prospects "the Oriole way."

Despite his early recall from Rochester, Cal was voted Rookie of the Year in the International League and was named to the loop's All-Star team at 3rd base. He was also voted top major league prospect by the IL's managers and coaches.

Brutal travel made Cal Sr. largely an absentee father to his three sons and daughter. But his wife Violet, or just plain Vi, with beautiful black hair and piercing blue eyes, was completely devoted. Every year, as soon as school was out, she packed up the brood and went rolling down the interstates in search of her husband.

"ALL OF MY CHILDREN WERE BLESSED WITH GOOD PHYSICAL DEVELOPMENT AT A YOUNG AGE, BUT BEING SUBJECTED TO BASEBALL THROUGH THEIR FATHER GAVE CAL AND BILL A LITTLE EXTRA LOVE FOR THE GAME, A LITTLE EXTRA INCENTIVE."

Vi Ripken

Cal Sr.'s profession may have had its price on his family, but it also had a profound impact. During those summers, and at tender ages, two of his sons were already discovering their life's work.

"All of my four children were blessed with good physical development at a young age," Vi Ripken remembered. "But being subjected to baseball through their father gave Cal and Bill a little extra love for the game, a little extra incentive."

In 1976, after 14 years of professional ball in the minors, Cal Sr. made his first appearance at The Show. He was finally in the Big Leagues. But even as he was unpacking his gear at Memorial Stadium, the most extraordinary talent he would ever develop was sitting in his own living room up in Aberdeen. Though at the time, very few people realized it.

"Cal Jr. was always hanging around the ballpark in those days," Brooks Robinson recalled. "His father would bring him and he'd stand out there all the time shagging fly balls. But I had no idea that I was looking at a future Hall of Famer. He just seemed like all the other kids, mine included, who were out there having fun."

Even that old molder of men, Cal Sr., didn't know what he had on his hands. "Nobody is smart enough to see a future Major Leaguer in a young teenager," he said. "Baseball is a game of adjustments. A player has to adjust at every level to succeed. Anyone could see that Cal had certain basic tools, but then a lot of young players have great physical assets and never make it. No one could have known back then that Cal would do everything right to get to the big leagues, let alone make the necessary adjustments to be such a success."

The larval Cal Ripken Jr. may not have seemed too different from other gifted young players at

49

Cal was recalled from Rochester on August 8, 1981. He made his big league debut as a pinch runner on August 10 for Ken Singleton in Baltimore against the Royals.

first, but it wasn't long before he was separating himself quite conspicuously. In fact, as he progressed through high school, he developed into something of a prodigy. His senior-year accomplishments were incredible in their scope. He won the Harford County batting title with a .492 average. If it were possible, he was even more impressive from the pitcher's mound where he made opposing batsmen seem like suckers as he posted a 7-2 record with a 0.70 ERA.

In fact, most Major League scouts looking in his direction were inclined to see a serious pitching prospect.

But it was the Orioles who selected him in 1978's spring amateur draft, and

At Aberdeen High School (Maryland), class of '78, Cal both pitched and played shortstop. He was 7-2 with a 0.70 ERA as a senior with 100 strikeouts in 60 innings.

they had something different in mind. Just one year earlier, the most important figure in franchise history had walked away. After more than 22 seasons, Brooks

Fans often witnessed this familiar sight at Memorial Stadium. Here, father and son concentrate on batting practice.

Cal's always been interested in baseball. As a kid, he played Little League, Babe Ruth, and Mickey Mantle League baseball. In fact, he led the Putty Hill, Maryland team to the Mickey Mantle World Series in Sherman, Texas.

Robinson retired. The organization was almost certainly fantasizing about a successor when they projected the then lanky and long-haired Ripken as a third baseman.

Of course, thanks to Earl Weaver, Cal was neither pitcher nor third baseman.

"Everybody in the organization was sure Cal was a natural third baseman," Brooks Robinson said. "Only Earl insisted he would be a great shortstop. So Earl held his ground and eventually got his own way."

Perhaps Brooks considered his own enduring reputation as baseball's greatest third baseman when he laced this thought with a hint of laughter: "I'm pretty glad Earl made him a shortstop," he said.

Of course Cal Jr. wasn't just a shortstop. He was the shortstop on his father's team in the Major Leagues.

During Cal's early years, he had a lot of fun on the team, playfully harassing visiting club's mascots with teammate Eddie Murray.

AFTER MORE THAN 22 SEASONS, BROOKS ROBINSON RETIRED. THE ORGANIZATION WAS ALMOST CERTAINLY FANTASIZING ABOUT A SUCCESSOR WHEN THEY PROJECTED THE THEN LANKY AND LONG-HAIRED RIPKEN AS A THIRD BASEMAN.

Those were heady days for father and son, a time when it seemed one thrill only lead to another. In 1982, the Orioles engineered a late-season miracle comeback that left them tied with Milwaukee on the next-to-last day. Only on the

A popular twosome, Cal and Eddie Murray both received honors by being selected as Most Valuable Orioles for the 1983 season.

very last day of the season did their luck run out. Nevertheless, the year was a triumph for Cal Jr. Batting just in front of the great Eddie Murray, he belted 28 homers and was named Rookie of the Year.

There was no way 1983 could possibly be as good. So it was even better. Baltimore won both the pennant and World's Championship, and Cal was the very best the American League had to offer. In just his second season, he was voted Most Valuable Player.

When news came, soon after, that yet another Ripken was entering the Orioles system, the baseball world seemed the family's personal Chesapeake Bay oyster.

Then — in 1986 — a dream came true. A weary Earl Weaver was stepping down after his second tenure as manager. His handpicked replacement would be his longtime confidant, friend and third base coach — Calvin Edwin Ripken Sr.

Cal and Billy Ripken played a total of 663 games together. They started in 634 games and turned 287 double plays.

Just as Cal Jr. was reaching his prime as one of the game's greats, Cal Sr. was receiving the recognition his loyalty and talents demanded. The true pinnacle, however, wouldn't come until mid-season when the Birds recalled a second base prospect from Rochester. His name was Billy Ripken.

For the first time in big league history a father was managing two of his sons.

"I remember thinking at the time how special it was to have three members of the family on the same team," Vi said. "I felt really good about it."

Cal Sr., unsentimental and ever the professional, found nothing unusual about having two sons on his team. "I had already been a manager in the minor leagues for more than 14 years," he said. "In that time I came to regard all of the boys as my sons. Cal and Billy were just two more. They had a job to do and I had a job to do."

And, oh, how well they performed those jobs! Though scouting reports for Billy weren't nearly as flattering as they had been for Cal, he shared at least one quality with his big brother. He knew how to handle a glove.

Billy Ripken was nothing short of spectacular afield. And in the organization of Robinson, Aparicio, Belanger, Blair, Grich, Murray and Cal Ripken, that

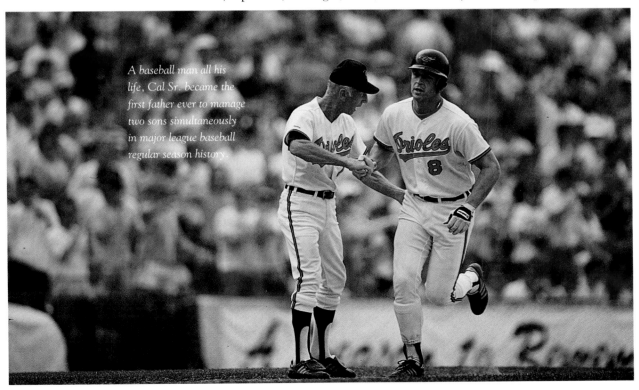

A baseball man all his life, Cal Sr. became the first father ever to manage two sons simultaneously in major league baseball regular season history.

meant quite a bit. Still, fans could be excused if at first they didn't believe Billy really was a Ripken. He seemed so different from his father and brother. Cal smashed homers; Billy slapped singles. Cal played the field

Billy Ripken's fielding techniques were often remarkable. In personality, he appeared different from both his father and his brother. He was the jokester, always making others laugh. Yet his approach to the game was very much like the elder Ripkens, passionate and determined.

effortlessly, making even the most difficult plays routine. Billy made the ordinary extraordinary, flinging his body right or left and stealing base hits in the web of his magical mitt.

THE RIPKEN BOYS PLAYED SIDE BY SIDE FOR MORE THAN FIVE YEARS. FROM 1987 THROUGH 1992, THEY WERE THE MOST PROLIFIC SIBLING DOUBLE-PLAY COMBINATION IN HISTORY, TURNING 287 TWIN KILLINGS.

Nowhere did their differences seem more pronounced, however, than in the simple contrasts of their personalities. Cal Jr., like his father, was stoic. The two elder Ripkens took a serious workman-like approach to a game they regarded with solemn earnestness. Billy was a clowning, rough-housing, passionate, diving, head-first sliding jokester.

He wasn't a natural like Cal, and that led to hurtful and unfair charges of nepotism. In fact, Billy was a competent and, at times, even spectacular Major Leaguer. He sparked the team with his inspired play, and his defensive numbers speak for themselves.

Though he was sometimes denigrated as a liability at the plate, Billy could be quite productive. In 1990, he even out-hit Cal, batting a highly respectable .291. He also tied for the American League lead with 17 sacrifices.

The Ripken boys played side by side for more than five years. From 1987 through 1992, they were the most prolific sibling double-play combination in history, turning 287 twin killings. A case could even be made that they were one of the best shortstop/second base compliments ever, even compared to those that didn't share DNA. In 1990, the two made just 11 combined errors for the entire season, the least ever allowed by a major league duo.

Perhaps it seemed the good times would last forever. Of course, they could not. In the game of baseball, the same man who was a national hero in his early twenties is usually a washed-up old codger by his mid-thirties. It is a society where all things are accelerated. And so it was that the Ripken dynasty waned as suddenly as it had risen. In 1988, Cal Sr. was painfully relieved as manager. He was eventually rehired — to his old position as third-base coach — but following the '92 season, he was released again. Not long after, so was Billy.

Cal Jr. has often described this period as the most disappointing of his career. How could it have been otherwise? The Ripkens lived something that almost

Defensively, Cal and Bill accounted for a total of only 11 errors in 1990, the fewest errors in major league history by a qualifying keystone combination. Offensively, the brothers Ripken combined for 335 home runs in the major leagues (13 by Billy). This figure ranks the two 9th among all-time brother combinations.

Two different teams.
Two different positions.
Two different players.
Same last name.
Cal and Billy
in 1993.

every American father and his sons dream about. Had it lasted fifty years, it would have been all too brief. For his few regrets, Cal Ripken Jr. finds tremendous comfort in the family he has built with his wife, Kelly. The two were married in 1987, though theirs was not the typical attraction. Kelly admits that she didn't even know who the hometown hero was when she first met him. As for his fascination with her, well it wasn't exactly stirred by the usual assets.

"He was interested in my height," Kelly remembered, laughing. "He wanted to be sure I was good material for producing basketball players."

Cal and Kelly Ripken enjoy
Family Day at Memorial
Stadium in 1990 with
daughter Rachel.

The non-stop shortstop was more interested in producing the next Michael Jordan than Mickey Mantle.

The happy ending is, Cal and Kelly now have two children. Five-year old Rachel and two-year old Ryan fill up their Worthington Valley home. And at an age when most toddlers can only dribble Gerbers, Ryan has already shown great potential on the hardwood — at least according to his doting mother.

Cal is a hoops fan — he plays basketball at his home and makes frequent visits to the USAir Arena.

And of Cal's other family — the Baltimore community he adopted so long ago when his career was just beginning — Cal still cares for them. He takes his commitments very seriously, and contributes in a number of ways to improve life in the city.

Cal and Kelly's cause of greatest concern, the one to which they devote the bulk of their time and resources, is literacy. Funds donated by the Kelly and Cal Ripken Jr. Foundation established and maintain The Ripken Learning Center, a program of Baltimore Reads. The facility helps adults with low reading skills learn with dignity so that they can find both personal fulfillment and better career opportunities.

At a time when some athletes proudly proclaim in television commercials, "I am not a role model," Cal Ripken offers Baltimore's adult students much more than just money, he offers them an example.

"Cal gets up to bat practically every inning of every game, because he understands the value of hard work," said Maggi G. Gaines, Executive Director of Baltimore Reads. "Adult learners respect that, because they also have to be dedicated."

Dedication. That's what makes a man show up for a demanding job every single day for 14 years. And it's also what makes him a successful member of a family.

In 1989, Cal and Kelly Ripken contributed $250,000 to the City of Baltimore to establish The Ripken Learning Center. This adult literacy program serves 240 students within Baltimore City. Then, in 1991, Cal established the Reading, Runs and Ripken program again in conjunction with Baltimore Reads, Inc., which raises money for literacy programs in Baltimore through donations based on the number of home runs Cal hits during a season.

Students at the Ripken Learning Center learn important reading skills.

Then-Maryland Governor William Donald Schaefer presented a proclamation on behalf of the citizens of Maryland to Cal Jr. for his outstanding commitment to the game of baseball both on and off the field. Kelly, Vi, and Cal Sr. enjoy the moment.

"Cal has always made it very clear to me that — in his book — family is first, family's number one," Kelly Ripken said. "When he's home, he loves to spend time with his children."

And does the hardest working baseball player of all time do his part around the house?

"Of course," she said. "He changes dirty diapers if that's what you mean." ■

"He is the most respected man in baseball."

~ BRADY ANDERSON ~

Chapter 6

"Baseball God"

BY
ANTHONY VERNI

CAL RIPKEN JR. "Baseball God." Few players in a generation deserve this lofty title. Few players have been on the verge of surpassing one of the most unbreakable records in the history of baseball. Few players have earned this label more than Baltimore Orioles shortstop Cal Ripken Jr.

He is one of the best shortstops to ever grace a baseball diamond. Thomas Boswell, columnist for *The Washington Post*, wrote that Ripken is the greatest shortstop in American League history. *Sports Illustrated* named him the shortstop on its All-Time Dream Team. His statistics, records, and awards speak volumes about his offensive and defensive skills. Opposing teams in the American League are all too familiar with Ripken beating them with both his bat and glove. The National Leaguers have seen him show off his skills in the last 13 consecutive All-Star Games and the 1983 World Series. They are lucky they're in the National League and don't have to face Ripken on a regular basis.

Since he joined the Orioles in 1981, Ripken has been a symbol of everything that is good about baseball. It is nearly impossible to find anyone affiliated with America's pastime who does not have the utmost respect and admiration for him as a player and person. The people who have the best understanding of how special Ripken is are those who watch and work with him every day.

On the field, what makes Ripken so valuable and separates him from other shortstops are what the numbers do not show. Orioles broadcaster John

Lowenstein remarks, "Cal is a fabulously inventive player. If things aren't going well at the plate or in the field, he makes the adjustments that are necessary to straighten those things out." Orioles pitcher Kevin Brown, who faced Ripken while with the Texas Rangers, says, "He's a very intelligent hitter. You have to mix pitches up on him. You can't fall into any kind of pattern with him. He'll take advantage of you."

The average baseball fan is well aware of Ripken's hitting prowess. Those who watch him regularly are even more impressed with his masterful defense. "On defense, Cal is bigger than life," says Lowenstein. And no one appreciates Ripken's name etched in stone on the line-up card more than Orioles pitchers. "It's been great having him play behind me," says Brown. "He's a very consistent, very good defensive player day in and day out. He always seems to be in the right spot. When the ball is hit up the middle, it seems like he is shading the guy that way. If he hits it in the hole, he's over there." Ripken's fielding is "golden." He's won two Gold Glove Awards. He should have more. Orioles Hall of Fame third baseman Brooks Robinson (and Ripken's idol) believes, "Nobody plays shortstop like he does. Nobody puts as much thought into playing the position. He's the best I've ever seen when it comes to playing the hitters." Orioles infielder, Jeff Huson states, "His knowledge of the hitters and the game is unbelievable. He knows about hitters and positioning better than anyone I ever played with or against." To make matters worse for opposing batters, Ripken has one of the strongest and most accurate arms in baseball. Longtime Orioles broadcaster Chuck Thompson comments, "I often think, 'That's a heck of a play, but he's not gonna be able to throw the runner out.' Yet he does."

Ripken's impact on the Orioles goes far beyond his consistent offensive and defensive play. His daily presence makes the team better. "In a sense, he is more

Two of the greatest Orioles share a moment on-field during the final weekend at Memorial Stadium. Cal often remarks that Brooks has always been his idol.

Orioles coach Elrod Hendricks has said that Cal's role is often more important than a coach's role. "The players are sometimes afraid to come to the coaches. It's easier for the young players to go to a player that they respect like Cal," he said.

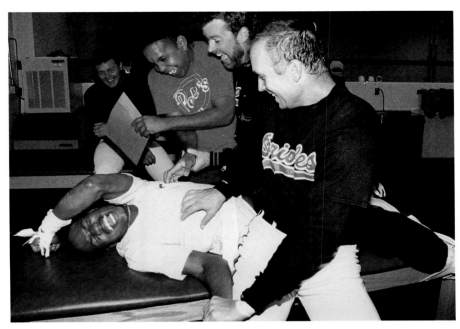

important than a coach," says Elrod Hendricks, Orioles coach and former catcher. "The players are sometimes afraid to come to the coaches. It is easier for the young players to go to a player that they respect like Cal." It is clear that Ripken is not a verbal "cheerleader." He leads by example. Both young and veteran teammates believe he is invaluable to the

Fun and games behind the scenes? In a photo from 1992, Mark Parent, Orioles clubhouse assistant Butch Burnett, Rick Sutcliffe, and Cal all tickle Oriole batboy Ivan Crayton.

Orioles. One doesn't have to look too far to find Ripken serving as the leader on the club. According to Orioles catcher Chris Hoiles, "He has helped me out a lot, just talking to me in different situations. He is always there, always willing to listen, always available to talk, always willing to help. That's Cal." When first sharing the infield with Ripken, third baseman Jeff Manto admits he was initially star struck by the future Hall of Famer. However, he gladly accepts guidance, noting, "Cal is always communicating on the field. He helps set me up defensively and has been a great asset for me." Rookie centerfielder, Curtis Goodwin, compares playing with Ripken to his stint with basketball legend Michael Jordan in the Arizona Fall League. "Cal's a big-time idol like Jordan. The first time I threw to Cal from the outfield, I got kind of scared." Goodwin laughs, "He teased me, saying I was throwing cutters at him."

Does Ripken experience pain? Absolutely. Nagging injuries? Yes. But they don't stop him. Nothing does. "He seems to have the ability to block out pain

John Lowenstein, who played with Ripken, comments, "Cal is a fabulously inventive player. If things aren't going well at the plate or in the field, he makes the adjustments that are necessary to straighten those things out."

and discomfort, whether physical, mental, or emotional when the umpire yells 'Play Ball,'" says Orioles strength and conditioning coach Tim Bishop. To be at the top of his game, Ripken is committed to remain in outstanding physical condition. "I think I am most impressed with his work habits. He is the most consistent and does the most activity in the off-season of anybody in the organization. I see other players watch him, watch what he does, especially in the winter time. He is an

Rookie players and those new to the club look up to Cal and heed his advice. Jeff Manto and Manny Alexander talk with Cal during an inning break.

excellent role model for all of our players, especially younger guys coming up," Bishop said. Don't ask Ripken for a grand tour of the trainer's room. He can't be too familiar with it. He frequents it only to have his ankles taped prior to a game. Trainer and friend Jamie Reed explains, "Everything we do for him is preventative. That's the way he looks at things because he stays in shape to prevent getting hurt. Cal has a totally different mental approach than just about everybody else." Former teammate and current coach Mike Flanagan points out that, when it comes to work ethic, "Cal goes one step beyond everyone. That is his barometer for what a good day's work is. When we play basketball in the winter, after everyone stops, he plays for another five minutes. That's the way he is."

Cal's work ethic is admired by those who know him. "He is the most consistent and does the most activity in the off-season of anybody in the organization," says Tim Bishop

The Streak. Since May 30, 1982, over 3,700 major league players have gone on the disabled list. Ripken has not missed a single game in that time. And he plays the most demanding position on the field, next to catcher. "On a day that Cal is tired, he pushes himself even more, which is sort of a throwback to the players from when I came along," remarks Elrod Hendricks. "Some players have the slightest ache or tiredness and they are ready to come out of the line-up. There are not too many players, young or old, that want to play every day like Cal."

The Streak amazes teammates. Pitcher Ben McDonald recently said, "He gets hit by a 90 mile-per-hour fastball and won't bruise. I nicknamed him the Karate Man because he never bruises on the outside, only on the inside. He heals a lot faster than the rest of us. He's not normal. Athletes like that come along once in a blue moon."

Through it all — pain, nagging injuries, and fatigue — Cal has an amazing commitment to the game, his teammates, and his fans!

The Streak inspires teammates. "It makes you want to come out and play even harder because he has played through injuries, slumps, you name it and he's done it. If he can do it, we should be able to come out and give it all we've got," says first baseman Rafael Palmeiro. Curtis Goodwin now believes that, "If you get to a point in your game when you feel tired, you just look at Cal and say 'I can't be tired.'" Leftfielder Brady Anderson recalls a humorous anecdote from last season. "I remember when I had a pinched nerve in my neck and had trouble turning to

see the pitcher. I went to the trainer and said, 'What am I going to do about this?' He said, 'You don't think Cal has had a few pains in his neck in the last 12 years?'" Anderson, a close friend of Ripken's, says, "I've learned a lot about dedication, desire, and what it takes to want to play every day from Cal."

Perhaps Thomas Boswell's outlook on Ripken and The Streak is most insightful. He wrote, "Don't ask if Ripken can break Lou Gehrig's record of 2,130 consecutive games played. That's thinking small. Ask if he can play 2,500 in a row."

Ripken believes he has a responsibility to the fans, community, and media who have supported him throughout his career. In a perfect world, all sports figures would be like Cal Ripken Jr. Humble. Professional. Dedicated. A friend of the fans. Manto

"IF YOU GET TO A POINT IN YOUR GAME WHEN YOU FEEL TIRED, YOU JUST LOOK AT CAL AND SAY 'I CAN'T BE TIRED.'"

Cal looks over his kingdom.

says, "You hear about players always portrayed as spoiled rotten kids that don't respond to the fans. Then you come over here and see Cal Ripken and you finally see a superstar who has time for the fans." As many know, it is not uncommon to see Ripken signing autographs for an hour or two after a game at Oriole Park or on the road. To illustrate Ripken's loyalty to baseball fans, Orioles public relations director, John Maroon, tells a story that occurred at this year's All-Star Game festivities at The Ballpark in Arlington. "I was dragging him from media interview to media interview in 105-degree heat. Finally he said, 'Let's take a break.' For the next hour and a half, his idea of a break was standing by the railing taking pictures with people and signing autographs. Afterward, he got a huge ovation from the fans as he walked off the field. He continually goes above and beyond the call of duty."

Orioles fans are well aware of Ripken's community service. However, there are the "little" things that few know about. "People don't realize how often Cal is called upon for community programs," says Julie Wagner, Orioles director of

A powerful player in his own right, Palmeiro has said that Cal's streak "makes you want to play even harder because he has played through injuries, slumps, you name it and he's done it. If he can do it, we should be able to come out and give it all we've got."

Ripken's teammates congratulate him on a grand slam against the Oakland A's on June 3, 1995.

community relations, who has been working with Ripken since 1982. "When he does something, he gives it his all. He often meets sick children before a game without any fanfare. Cal does it because he is a good guy. He sits and talks with the kids. Cal is always polite and they love him."

Closing in on Lou Gehrig's record, media demand for Ripken has increased dramatically this season. John Maroon works closely with Ripken to handle all the requests for interviews. "We have a press conference on the first day into every city on the road to answer media questions regarding The Streak," says Maroon. "Cal understands it is his obligation as an athlete. The press loves to deal with him because he is ultra professional. He answers the same questions every time with a smile on his face. He realizes when he talks to someone, even though it is the same question, it's asked by a different person."

Chris Hoiles (left) with Mike Mussina and Cal after an Orioles victory. "He has helped me out a lot, just talking to me in different situations. He is always there, always willing to help. That's Cal," says Hoiles.

Cal Ripken Jr. and baseball are synonymous. He has always been a fan of the game he plays. It shows. He respects the game. The feeling is mutual. As Brady Anderson states, "He is the most respected man in baseball by the fans and players." Longtime *Baltimore Sun* columnist John Steadman wrote, "The mere mention of Cal Ripken Jr. represents the personification of excellence."

Perhaps this is why Rafael Palmeiro called Cal Ripken a "Baseball God." Indeed he is. ■

"Just look at Cal. There's someone to emulate."

~ JIM PALMER ~

Chapter 7

Local Hero

BY
MARY HUGHES

A MOMENTARY ENCOUNTER with a legend, no matter how brief, is something never to be forgotten. Meeting a hero for the first time — even if only shaking a hand, receiving an autograph, or seeing the person from a distance — can be an intensely personal experience. Just about everyone has such a story about his or her idol.

Buddy Kerr's moment came when he encountered Lou Gehrig, a man forever to be remembered as one of the greatest ever to play the game of baseball. Kerr, now a scout for the New York Yankees, was a teenager on a tryout with the team that made Gehrig a legend. His story:

"I was working out with the Yankees. In those days they had a uniform for you, you put it on, and they told you to go sit in the dugout and wait for the other ballplayers. Nobody got there for at least an hour. I was the only one there.

"I saw the fence open in center field and a man came in and started walking across the field toward the dugout. He was in street clothes and he looked to be an old man because of the way he was walking." Buddy illustrates with his hands close together, the slow shuffle, the painfully slow gait of the man coming in from center field. "When he reached the dugout and was ready to go down the steps, he grabbed the railing. By then I knew who he was. I went over to help him down the three steps into the dugout, because I was afraid he was going to fall. But he looked at me and said, 'It's okay, Red, I'm alright.' I guess my hair was a little reddish in color, so he called me 'Red.'

"He was exhausted by the walk in from the outfield, so he sat down to catch his breath. We talked for a few minutes. He looked at my glove — and I was excited about having Lou Gehrig look at my glove — and said, 'I guess you'll be needing a new glove soon.' I thought my glove was still pretty good, but he told me, 'I'll see if "Crow" (Frankie Crosetti) doesn't have a glove for you.'

"Every day, I'd suit up, sit on the bench, waiting for the other ballplayers, and he'd come in from behind the center field fence, sit on the bench and talk to me. That went on for about two weeks. On the last day, he said to me, 'I guess you think I forgot about that glove, don't you, Red?'" Kerr smiles at the memory, then runs his hand through his hair, now sparse and white. "Gehrig said, 'You go see Pop Logan — the equipment manager — after the game. He'll have a glove for you.' And he did. He gave me the glove."

Buddy Kerr has had many interesting experiences throughout his baseball career, but he remembers particularly his personal brush with a legend, Lou Gehrig.

Many Orioles fans have had a similar brush with a legend. Not the heroic Yankee first baseman, but a man who shares his legendary work ethic, Cal Ripken Jr. They, too, have stories to tell about Baltimore's favorite shortstop. There are those fans who have met Cal, those who know of him, those who know someone who knows him, or those who admire him from afar. Each encounter, in its own way, is personal. Together, they all are special in helping

Cal's been a hometown favorite ever since he stepped onto the field at Memorial Stadium in 1981.

The consecutive game streak record; the consecutive All-Star game elections; and the two Gold Gloves make Cal a favorite player not only to the fans, but also to the media.

Opening Week 1992 brought many exciting festivities to Oriole Park and the downtown area. A parade down Pratt Street was one of the highlights. Cal and then-Governor William Donald Schaefer rode in a car together.

tell the story of a baseball phenomenon and local hero named Cal Ripken Jr.

Here, then, are the stories of Cal's fans...

Scott Norton: "When I was a little kid, Cal Ripken Jr. gave me a bat. I was proud of the special souvenir. I walked through the stadium, hugging the bat. When a stranger asked to see it, I reluctantly handed over the bat to him. The stranger took off with it. I started screaming at the top of my lungs, and others soon responded, chasing down the bat-nabber and returning it back to me, eternally grateful.

"Years later, working in a production company that sometimes does work for the Orioles, I crossed paths with Cal Ripken Jr. again when he visited my office. I showed Ripken that I still had the bat he had given me and I relayed the story of how I almost lost it. Cal asked if he could take a look at it and I handed it to the man who had originally given it to me.

"Cal turned the old bat over and over in his hands, smiling as he noticed the number 8 scrawled on the knob of the bat. 'I'd forgotten that I used to write that,' he said, as he swung the old bat several times before handing it back to me. You could tell how just holding that bat brought back fond memories for him."

David Wayne Baldwin Jr. ,7, has a purple plastic Dino the Dinosaur that came out of a Fruity Pebbles cereal box. Two years ago, David had Dino autographed by Cal Ripken Jr. According to David's dad, the dinosaur has never been lost, simply because David takes it everywhere. David can be seen clutching the dinosaur at Orioles home games. Incidentally, Cal signed the dinosaur in purple.

Meghan McInnes is a little reluctant to admit it, but her father, Tom, reports: "We rode our bikes to his house, every day for a while, but we couldn't get past

GAME 1,999: Prince's song entitled "1999" was played and it didn't take long for the fans to respond. Cal received a standing ovation and acknowledged the hometown crowd.

"CAL'S REAL. THAT'S WHY HE WAS THE #1 VOTE GETTER FOR THE ALL-STAR GAME. PEOPLE KNOW HE'S REAL."

the gate. Actually, we watched his house being built." Dad continues, "Cal is someone to look up to in Baltimore. A great role model for the kids."

Chris Burns of Bel Air, MD, got Cal Ripken Jr.'s autograph, but, he laments, he doesn't have it anymore. "It was at Memorial Stadium. I waited a long time to get that autograph — I was probably five when I got it," he said. "Cal signed my shorts, and my mom washed them."

John Degen of Tacoma Park, MD, claims, "I saw Cal Ripken's first game at Memorial Stadium...I was also in the movie, Major League II. I got to stand on the infield. I didn't want to wash my shoes after that. I carried them around, showing them to everybody. Everyone was impressed. That's the same dirt Cal Ripken stands on!"

Henrietta Wolf of Dallastown, PA, and her two nieces told a story. As the three women sat on the third base side one Sunday afternoon, they insisted that their Aunt Henrietta is Cal's biggest fan. Henrietta's snow white hair was neatly tucked under her patriotic stars and stripes ball cap. She proudly showed off her

Boggs' and Ripken's names continually show up on All-Star ballots year after year. These two have played in their share of All-Star games.

Cal Ripken tee-shirt, given to her by her nieces. "I have to wear my Cal shirt because our birthdays are the same — not the same year — but the same date — August 24th. I always send Cal a birthday card, and he sends me pictures of himself in his uniform. He sent me three pictures last year!"

Karl M. Ferron, a photographer for the *Baltimore Sun*, saw a side of Cal Ripken Jr. that most people don't see. "There was a patient over at John Hopkins Hospital. The child was really ill, so weak that they had to pull him around in a wagon. Cal went over to him and asked what his name was. The next thing I know, Cal's over there, writing an autograph on a photograph for the kid — he turns his hat backwards and is chatting with this kid! The boy was weak, but you could tell in his eyes that Cal had touched him."

Phil Wood of WTEM Radio has been the official scorer at many Orioles games this season. He's known Cal for a while now and figures, "He owes me about 75 cents. He used to bum quarters off reporters so he could play pinball over at the old ballpark. He never paid me back. I figure with interest — this happened in about 1976 — he owes me about 1.6 million dollars. Other than that, it seems that every time I'm official scorer and there's a hit that's questionable, it involves Cal."

Does Phil let that 75 cents sway his judgment when he's determining whether the play in question should be ruled a hit or an error?

"I try not to," he says kiddingly.

Told about Phil Wood's story, former Orioles outfielder John Lowenstein, now a broadcaster for HTS/O's TV, has an immediate comeback. "Cal doesn't owe me any money." Then he laughs and laments, "I wish he did!"

"AS A PLAYER YOU TAKE OFF A DAY HERE AND THERE – MAYBE ONE DAY A MONTH – AND IT REALLY HELPS. HE HASN'T TAKEN A DAY OFF IN 14 YEARS."

Two familiar and well-respected individuals share a moment on Opening Day 1994 — owner Peter Angelos and Number 8.

Former Oriole Eddie Murray deserves credit for helping Cal become an everyday player. Having celebrated his own remarkable accomplishment, his 3,000th base hit earlier this year, Murray had this to say about Cal and The Streak: "It's something special — to play that many games and not really be hurt. The other thing is not to have any illnesses in the family or other interruptions. I've missed a couple of games due to that. You have to take your hat off to the man for not being sick— and he has been — but he's still gone out and performed."

Mike Klein, an Orioles "Designated Hitter," smiles and says, "In 1991 at the All-Star game I had a pass. I was in the basement of the Skydome, and I took a picture of Cal on a golf cart holding the MVP trophy. It's a one-of-a-kind photograph because it's just Cal and the trophy — all by himself."

Pete Ballard of Rochester, NY, claims, "I can remember seeing him play in Rochester. My brother and I got a Cal Ripken home run ball because at Silver Stadium, we knew where to go behind the fence." He said, "Cal hit the home run over the right field fence where there's a gap between the

All-Star Week in 1993 featured FanFest at the Baltimore Convention Center, a baseball theme park with memorabilia and interactive attractions. The consummate All-Star shortstop was prominently featured.

There's no denying it…the fans love their Baltimore shortstop.

fence and the billboard wall. My brother just picked up that home run ball and got Cal's autograph on it. He was only 6 or 7 at the time."

Jim Kuzma and his daughter, Mary Ann, sit on the third base side of the ballpark. Says Jim, "My daughter's in love with Cal. She has been for the past two or three years. We have season tickets just so she can come and watch him play." Dad's not kidding. Mary Ann's tuned in to the field, watching her favorite player, and she won't divert her eyes to answer a question. Most dads probably wouldn't want their daughter to be in love with a married man, but Jim doesn't seem too worried. He smiles, "She's five years old."

Karen Chapman relayed this touching story: "A friend of ours was in a serious car accident. He was hurt very badly. He was a major baseball fan, and just loved Cal. Cal went to visit him while he was in the hospital. It meant an awful lot." Karen reports that her friend has made a nice recovery since then.

Hank Meyer, age 6, of Baltimore, recalls (with help from his mom): "We flew from Baltimore to Florida the day after Thanksgiving. Mom, Dad, and I were in

Cal goes the extra mile, especially when it comes to meeting special friends.

Disney World waiting for a parade. Mom yelled, 'There's Cal Ripken.' He was sitting on the curb across the street with his little girl. Dad and I went over to say hello. We talked to Cal and Dad took my picture with him. He was a really nice guy. It was the neatest thing that happened on our vacation. The picture turned out so great we decided to use it as our Christmas card!"

Robby Shields of Catonsville, MD, con-tributed quite extensively to the Cal Ripken Jr. exhibit at the Babe Ruth Museum several years ago. He's a big fan of Cal's. He smiles when he relates that, "I had a sign that said, 'Cal Ripken —

World's Greatest Shortstop.' I was sitting behind home plate, and Kelly Ripken saw it, and she told me to come down and sit with her. I sat with her for two or three innings. When Cal won the MVP I had the same sign. Cal saw it and came over and shook my hand."

Joe Giza, a Reuters photographer, remembers: "I photographed Cal's first hit. All the photographers were trying to decide if he was going to connect or not. You know, was he there just because of his dad's connections or did he have what it takes to play in the major leagues. I can't remember what my opinion was at the time...I also remember when Cal got hit in the head. The next day, I took pho-tographs in the clubhouse of his batting helmet. There was an indentation in the helmet. You could see the complete impression of a baseball right there in the hel-met. That's endurance."

Even the young fans know that Cal's message over the years has been a strong one: 1) work hard, 2) keep reading, and 3) drink your milk!

Hank Meyer, age 6, will always have this special momento of his run-in with Cal in Florida.

79

Hank Peters, former Orioles General Manager, presents Cal with the 1982 Rookie of the Year Award.

Claudia, who wishes to remain "just Claudia," also has a Cal connection: "Do you know the guy who put in my mother's new kitchen cabinets actually went to high school with Cal Ripken?"

Richard Vatz of Cockeysville, MD, recalls, "I saw Cal play in a charitable basketball game at my daughter's school. That was about 10 years ago. It was the Orioles vs. the faculty. The thing that I remember most was Cal's intensity. He played hard. Sometimes these games can be a little silly, but he was serious. The faculty never stood a chance."

Norman and Tricia Snyder of Mt. Airy, MD, report that, "Our daughter is a big fan of Cal's and begged us to buy her the Orioles uniform so she could wear it for Halloween."

Finally, perhaps it takes one to know one when it comes to assessing the local hero that Cal Ripken has become. Jim Palmer. Heard the name?

"I looked for someone on the team to emulate when I first started in Baltimore. I decided I wanted to conduct myself as Brooks Robinson did," said the Orioles all-time winningest pitcher, who still lives in the area and broadcasts the team's games on television. Palmer directs his attention toward a scene taking place between the Orioles dugout and the backstop: hundreds of fans are pressing against the rail, crying out for autographs. Standing poised before them all, working calmly, efficiently, smiling, talking to the fans, is Cal Ripken Jr., signing ball after ball, card after card.

"Just look at Cal," says Palmer quietly. "There's someone to emulate." ■

Over thirteen years and Cal hasn't missed a day of work.

Chapter 8

Career Timeline

BY
STEPHANIE
PARRILLO

Let's go back 13 years to 1982. During that year, Spain became a member of NATO, the Pope visited Liverpool and Coventry on the third day of his six-day British trip, and a popular television classic, Cheers, debuted. "Ebony and Ivory" by Paul McCartney and Stevie Wonder graced the airwaves. On May 30 of that year, third baseman Cal Ripken Jr. went 0 for 2 as the Toronto Blue Jays beat the Orioles 6-0.

That was game one of Cal Ripken Jr.'s consecutive game streak. He didn't know at the time that he eventually would be moved to short-stop or that he would end up chasing Lou Gehrig's consecutive game record. He probably also didn't know that he'd become one of the best shortstops the game has seen or that he'd stay with the Baltimore Orioles until now. He didn't know there'd be a beautiful ballpark built in downtown Baltimore on the site of the City's one-time railroad center. How could he know these things at the time? He was just a rookie. He was just beginning his major league career.

Now, 13 years later, it's a different story. Cal Ripken Jr. is more mature, polished, worldly. He's learned the game and

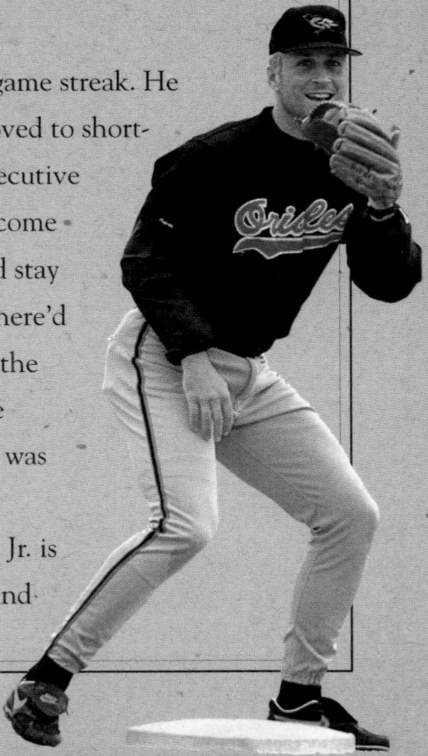

1981 ROCHESTER RED WINGS

continues to do so on a daily basis. He's become a master at his trade. Other players look up to him and seek his advice. Over 13 years and Cal hasn't missed a day of work. When you take a look back on all the events that have happened during that span, you realize exactly how much time has passed. There have been three different U.S. Presidents...the Berlin Wall has come down...Compact Discs have replaced vinyl albums...VCR's became a household item...and Michael Jackson continues to turn out hit albums. A lot has happened. Time marches on.

The following pages provide an account of Cal's career as each year progressed and as his consecutive game streak record began to mount. It's a great way to remember things that may have been forgotten. It's a great way to track the shortstop's career.

It's been a long haul when you focus on it and look at the days and the years that have passed.

It seems long to us, but not to Cal. He insists that it's his job and that when he comes to the ballpark, he comes to play. It's an amazing streak and proof of an incredible work ethic most of us wish we had ourselves. ■

Despite being called up to Baltimore August 8, 1981, Cal was voted Rookie of the Year in the International League for Rochester.

Cal Ripken Jr. from 1982 team photo, when The Streak began, to 1995 team photo.

82

NATIONAL ASSOCIATION OF PROFESSIONAL BASEBALL LEAGUES

Uniform Player Contract

Parties: The parties to this Uniform Player Contract are The Bluefield Baseball Club, Club, Hereinafter "Club," and Calvin Edwin Ripken, Jr., hereinafter "Player," whose permanent mailing address is 410 Clover Street, Aberdeen, Maryland 21001.

BALTIMORE ORIOLES PROFESSIONAL INDIVIDUAL REPORT

POSITION PLAYERS

PLAYER: RIPKEN, CALVIN EDWIN JR. POS. SS
CLUB: BALTIMORE LEAGUE AMERICAN 1st Yr Pro Ball 1978
ORGANIZATION: BALTIMORE
D.O.B. 8/24/60 HT. 6'4 WT. 215 B R T R RACE

PHYSICAL DESCRIPTION: Tall—Well built & strong-broad shoulders-strong arms & legs
Glasses: Yes ☐ No ☐
Contacts: Yes ☐ No ☐
KNOWN INJURY/ILLNESS: KNOW OF NONE

STRONG POINTS: HITTING - POWER - ARM - FIELDING - BASE RUNNING - INSTINCTS - MAKE-UP
WEAK POINTS: NONE

PLAYER	Present	Future
Hitting	6	7
Power	7	7
Speed	5	5
Arm	6	6
Field	6	6
Base Running	6	6

OVERALL EVALUATION: Highest Class 6 ML Type Prospect 7 Next Year ML
Help Orioles: YES Present: YES Future: YES
MAKEUP GRADE 8
MAKEUP COMMENTS: Good drive, Desire & Competitor. Excell. Hustler. Great attitude.

SUMMATION: HAD ANOTHER GOOD YEAR ALBEIT NOT GREAT YEAR BY HIS STANDARDS - FOR A SS HE PROBABLY HAS THE BEST OFFENSIVE STATS IN ONE ML BY FAR, BUT I THINK WE WOULD BE A MUCH MORE SOLID DEFENSIVE INF. WITH HIM AT THIRD - I KNOW HE LEADS THE LEAGUE IN A LOT OF DEPT. BUT HE ALSO HAS 3 GROUND BALL PITCHERS IN MACGREGOR, FLANAGAN, & BODDICKER - PLAYS THE HITTERS & THE COUNTS WELL, BUT HE DOESN'T HAVE THE PURE RANGE OF A SS - SIMILAR TO SMALLEY IN HIS EARLY YEARS.

Suggest we PITCH & DEFENSE this hitter as follows:
No. Games Seen: 22
PITCH HIM: LHP: JAM OFF THE PLATE - CHANGE RHP: FB UP & IN - BRK STUFF AWAY
FB DOWN & AWAY
DEFENSE HIM: O.F. SHADES TO LF - CF A LOT. INF. STRT. AWAY.

Is he a first ball hitter: No Is he bothered by: A. Breaking balls YES B. Change of speeds YES C. Close pitches YES
Does he hit & run: YES
Will he take extra base: YES
Is he a threat to steal the base: No If yes, drag: push:
Will he bunt for a base hit: No Should we Acquire: YES

AVE	G	AB	R	H	2B	3B	HR	RBI	GW RBI	BB	SO	SB
.288	133	604	81	145	30	1	21	70	12	66	57	3

PLAYER (Last) RIPKEN, CAL (First) CLUB BALTIMORE
SCOUT Bill Werle Date of Report SEP 6 1986

FORM NOS. SF#35/PDF #11H REV.12/81

PLAYER SIGN HERE: Calvin Edwin Ripken Jr.
Social Security Number
City and State: Aberdeen Maryland Zip 21001
Player's Home Address-Street and No.

Consent of Parents or Guardian

Parent-Guardian: Violet R. Ripken
CLUB DATE AND SIGN HERE: AS TO CLUB: Signed this 13th day of June A.D. 1978
Bluefield Baseball Club
By: James M. McLaughlin
Title: Authorized Signature

NATIONAL ASSOCIATION OF PROFESSIONAL BASEBALL LEAGUES

BALTIMORE ORIOLES PROFESSIONAL INDIVIDUAL REPORT

POSITION PLAYERS

RIPKEN, (Last) CALVIN (First) EDWIN JR. (Middle) POS. SS
BALTIMORE-ORIOLES LEAGUE AMERICAN
8/24/60 HT. 6'4 WT. 218 B R T R RACE 1st Yr Pro Ball 1978

PHYSICAL DESCRIPTION: Tall—Well built and strong-Broad shoulders-Strong arms and legs
Glasses: Yes ☐ No ☐
Contacts: Yes ☐ No ☐
KNOWN INJURY/ILLNESS: KNOW OF NONE

STRONG POINTS: HITTING - POWER - ARM - FIELDING -
WEAK POINTS: SPEED - LOST SOME RANGE -

	Present	Future			
Hitch	No		Bat Speed	6	
Pull	6		Alley	7	
To 1st Base	4.41		Line Drive	7	
Str.	6		1st-3rd 2nd-Hm.	5	
Range	6		Release		
Leads	5		Hands	7	
			Agility	6	
			Breaks		Instinc

OVERALL EVALUATION: Highest Class 6 ML Type Prospect 7 Next Year ML
Help Orioles: YES Present: YES Future: YES
MAKEUP GRADE 8

SUMMATION: APPEARED TO BE MORE TIRED & PRESSING THIS YEAR - LOOKED TO BE TRYING TO PULL TO MUCH & NOT GOING TO RF AS OFTEN - ALSO THOUGHT THERE WERE GRAND BALLS HE SHOULD HAVE GOTTEN TO BUT DIDN'T - LACKS THE REAL RANGE BUT DOES POSITION HIMSELF & PLAYS THE HITTERS - SHOULD BOUNCE BACK WITH BAT IN 1988

RIPKEN, CAL (First) CLUB BALTIMORE
Bill Werle Date of Report AUG. 26 1987

PROFESSIONAL INDIVIDUAL REPORT

PHYSICAL DESCRIPTION:
Glasses: Yes ☐ No ☐
Contacts: Yes ☐ No ☐
KNOWN INJURY/ILLNESS:

STRONG POINTS: GOOD OFFENSIVE PRODUCTION WITH GOOD TO EXCELLENT. ARM, SURE + ARM + FIELDER, SMART

SUMMATION: FRANCHISE PLAYER WITH JUST GREAT ... MAKE-UP & DEMEANOR. A PLEASURE TO ... EACH PLAY. PLAYED SS BETTER OVERALL ... THIS YR. THAN LAST. A VERY DURABLE ... PLAYER. PLAYS SMART. KNOWS LITTLE ... MAKES UP FOR OVERALL SPEED WITH ... SMARTS. QUICK & SURE HANDS. ... CONSISTENT PERFORMER YR IN + YR. OUT.

RIPKEN, CAL (First) CLUB BALT.
Bill Werle Date of Report 10-20-16

... POWER - ARM - FIELDING - MAKE ... INSTINCTS

... ALTHOUGH HE WILL END UP WITH ... NUMBERS THEY WON'T BE THE KIND ... CAPABLE OF PRODUCING AS FAR ... HOME RUNS & HIS RBI'S SHOW ... THERE BECAUSE OF HAVING ... LEGACY IN FRONT OF HIM - ... OF THE ASSISTS HE'LL ... I THINK THEY SHOULD BE ... THE OPPORTUNITIES HE'S ... BEEN A LITTLE CARELESS ... CONCENTRATING AS MUCH ... THIS YEAR -

Draft picks Ripken, Norris sign contracts with Orioles

1982

CALVIN EDWIN RIPKEN JR

Ripken Season Milestones

~ Cal wins the Rookie of the Year Award by Baseball Writers of
America (BBWAA)

~ Cal leads all big league rookies in doubles (32), homers (28),
RBI (93), and runs (90)

~ Cal leads the American League rookies in games (160),
at bats (598), and runs (90)

~ Cal earns his first major league stolen base the hard way:
he steals home (May 31 in Baltimore)

84

Season Stats

	YEAR	CAREER
Average	.264	.256
Games	160	183
At Bats	598	637
Runs	90	91
Hits	158	163
Doubles	32	32
Triples	5	5
Home Runs	28	28
RBI	93	93
Bases on Balls	46	47
Strikeouts	95	103
Stolen Bases	3	3
Errors	13	15

THE YEAR THAT WAS – 1982

The Academy Award for Best Picture is Gandhi.

Cal plays in his first M.L. Opening Day (his 24th major league game) and hits his first M.L. home run.

Joe Montana and the San Francisco 49ers defeat the Cincinnati Bengals in the Super Bowl.

The Los Angeles Lakers defeat the Philadelphia 76ers in the NBA Championship.

The U.S. is in a recession with unemployment at about 11 percent.

May 30: The Streak begins.

Democrats win congressional mid-term elections.

Pete Rose breaks Ty Cobb's record for lifetime base hits and Rickey Henderson sets a new standard for stolen bases in a season.

Nuclear freeze movement spreads throughout Europe and the United States.

July 1: Manager Earl Weaver moves Cal from 3rd base to shortstop.

Jimmy Connors wins both Wimbledon and the U.S. Open.

E.T. is the biggest movie of the age. It blows away previous box office records.

Top rated shows of the year are: 60 Minutes, Dallas, M*A*S*H, Magnum, P.I. and Dynasty. Late Night with David Letterman begins to catch on.

The Billboard #1 song of the year is "I Love Rock and Roll" by Joan Jett and the Blackhearts.

The St. Louis Cardinals beat the Milwaukee Brewers in the World Series.

Orioles' Ripken Named AL Rookie of the Year

1983

CALVIN EDWIN RIPKEN JR.

Ripken Season Milestones

~ Chosen American League MVP by the BBWAA

~ First ever to win back-to-back BBWAA "Rookie" and "MVP" awards

~ Shares Most Valuable Oriole honors with Eddie Murray

~ Chosen as "Player of the Year" by *The Sporting News*

~ Leads majors in hits (211) and doubles (47) — both club records

~ Leads the American League in runs (121)

Season Stats

	YEAR	CAREER
Average	.318	.288
Games	162	345
At Bats	663	1300
Runs	121	212
Hits	211	374
Doubles	47	79
Triples	2	7
Home Runs	27	55
RBI	102	195
Bases on Balls	58	105
Strikeouts	97	200
Stolen Bases	0	3
Errors	25	40

THE YEAR THAT WAS – 1983

Terms of Endearment with Shirley MacLaine, Debra Winger, and Jack Nicholson is the Oscar Winner for the year.

The final episode of M*A*S*H, after 11 years on the air, is viewed by 125 million people.

The Washington Redskins, led by Joe Theismann and John Riggins, defeat the Miami Dolphins in the Super Bowl.

The Billboard #1 song of the year is "Every Breath You Take," by the Police.

Cal has his second highest batting average (.318), topped only by his .323 in 1991.

Return of the Jedi, part three of George Lucas' Star Wars trilogy, is the year's #1 box office hit. Tootsie with Dustin Hoffman follows close behind.

Martina Navratilova enjoys one of the most dominant years in women's tennis.

In game 200 of the streak, Cal hits his second career grand slam off Oakland's Tim Conroy in the 4th inning of a 6-2 win over the A's at Memorial Stadium. Storm Davis was the winning pitcher.

Cal tops major league shortstops in assists (534).

Cal is awarded the Silver Slugger Trophy as the major league's best offensive shortstop.

Harold Washington is elected the first black mayor of Chicago.

The Baltimore Orioles defeat the Philadelphia Phillies in the World Series.

CAL RIPKEN

1984

Ripken Season Milestones

~ Leads all major league shortstops in home runs (27)

~ Plays every inning of every game for second straight season

~ Sets major league record for assists in one season (583)

~ Elected to start at shortstop for the American League in the All-Star Game

Season Stats

	YEAR	CAREER
Average	.304	.293
Games	162	507
At Bats	641	1941
Runs	103	315
Hits	195	569
Doubles	37	116
Triples	7	14
Home Runs	27	82
RBI	86	281
Bases on Balls	71	176
Strikeouts	89	289
Stolen Bases	2	5
Errors	26	66

THE YEAR THAT WAS – 1984

April 27 is Cal's 300th game of The Streak. He goes 2 for 5 with the winning run in the 11th inning of a 4-3 win over Texas at Baltimore.

Democratic nominee Walter Mondale selects Representative Geraldine Ferraro as the first woman vice-presidential nominee of a major party.

The Rev. Jesse Jackson is the first black presidential candidate to become a major force, receiving millions of votes in the Democratic primaries.

Larry Bird and the Boston Celtics conquer the Los Angeles Lakers for the NBA Championship.

The Best Picture Oscar goes to Amadeus.

The Los Angeles Raiders defeat the Washington Redskins in the Super Bowl.

In the Olympics, the top U.S. athletes are sprint- er/long jumper Carl Lewis, hurdler Edwin Moses, and gymnast Mary Lou Retton.

Miss America Vanessa Williams gives up her crown following publication of nude photographs.

The Billboard #1 song of the year is "Like A Virgin" by Madonna.

August 16, in Cal's 400th game, he goes 1 for 4 in an 8-1 loss to Oakland in Baltimore.

The biggest movie hits of 1984 were Ghostbusters, Indiana Jones and the Temple of Doom, Gremlins, and Beverly Hills Cop.

Big TV shows for the year are Dynasty, Dallas, The Cosby Show, 60 Minutes, and Family Ties.

Ronald Reagan wins an overwhelming re-election victory.

The Detroit Tigers beat the San Diego Padres in the World Series.

1985

Ripken Season Milestones

~ Has a career high 116 runs

~ For the third straight year, Cal leads all major league shortstops in home runs (26), RBI (110), double plays (123), and slugging percentage (.469)

~ Sets a club record for most GIDPs (32)

~ Extends his consecutive game streak to 603, a club record

Season Stats

	YEAR	CAREER
Average	.282	.290
Games	161	668
At Bats	642	2583
Runs	116	431
Hits	181	750
Doubles	32	148
Triples	5	19
Home Runs	26	108
RBI	110	391
Bases on Balls	67	243
Strikeouts	68	357
Stolen Bases	2	7
Errors	26	92

THE YEAR THAT WAS – 1985

The Oscar winner for Best Picture is Out of Africa.

The San Francisco 49ers defeat the Miami Dolphins in the Super Bowl.

The Los Angeles Lakers beat the Boston Celtics in the NBA championship.

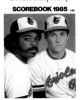

SCOREBOOK 1985

May 4: Cal surpasses Brooks Robinson to become the Orioles all-time leader in consecutive games played (game number 463). Cal goes 2 for 4 with a double and his third homer in as many games.

Rock groups record songs and raise millions to combat the mass starvation in Africa: USA for Africa, Band Aid, and the large Live Aid concert contributed.

June 15: Game 500 of The Streak, Cal goes 1 for 3 with a solo homer off Milwaukee's Bob Gibson in a 7-5 0's win at Memorial Stadium.

The most popular movie of the year is Back to the Future. Other popular films are Rambo, Rocky IV, Cocoon, and The Color Purple.

Boris Becker, at age 17, becomes the youngest Wimbledon champion in history.

Billboard's #1 song of the year is Lionel Richie's "Say You, Say Me."

The Cosby Show ranks high along with Family Ties, Murder, She Wrote, 60 Minutes, and Cheers. Miami Vice is a new addition to the tube.

Dwight Gooden has an historic pitching season.

The Kansas City Royals upset the St. Louis Cardinals in the World Series.

1986

CALVIN EDWIN RIPKEN JR

Ripken Season Milestones

~ Cal extends his consecutive game streak to 765, and consecutive innings to 6,937

~ For the fourth straight year, Cal leads major league shortstops in home runs (25), RBI (81), runs (98), and slugging percentage (.461)

~ Cal has his best defensive year thus far with .982 fielding percentage

~ Cal is elected for the third straight year to the All-Star Game

Season Stats

	YEAR	CAREER
Average	.282	.289
Games	162	830
At Bats	627	3210
Runs	98	529
Hits	177	927
Doubles	35	183
Triples	1	20
Home Runs	25	133
RBI	81	472
Bases on Balls	70	313
Strikeouts	60	417
Stolen Bases	4	11
Errors	13	105

THE YEAR THAT WAS – 1986

The Chicago Bears crush the New England Patriots in the Super Bowl.

Platoon wins the Best Picture Academy Award.

In January the space shuttle Challenger explodes after liftoff, killing its crew of seven, including schoolteacher Christa McAuliffe.

The #1 Billboard Song is "That's What Friends Are For" by Dionne Warwick and Friends.

Chris Evert Lloyd wins the French Open, her 14th consecutive Grand Slam tennis championship.

The Statue of Liberty's 100th birthday party is attended by nearly six million people while others across the country watched on television.

August 9: In his 741st game of his streak, Cal surpasses Dale Murphy for 11th all-time in consecutive games played.

Don Baylor of the Red Sox was hit by a pitch for the 25th time of the season, setting a new American League record.

The most talked about show of the year is Moonlighting. The Golden Girls is also a new hit show.

The Royal's 3-2 victory over the Brewer's extended Milwaukee's losing streak to a club record 11 games.

The year's top movie money makers include Top Gun, Crocodile Dundee, Aliens, and Star Trek 4: The Voyage Home.

The New York Mets come from behind to defeat the Boston Red Sox in the World Series.

Donruss '86

CAL RIPKEN JR. SS

1987

Ripken Season Milestones

~ Cal leads Orioles in RBI (98) for the first time

~ Cal draws a career high 81 walks

~ Cal leads the American League shortstops in assists (480)

~ Cal becomes the first American League shortstop to start four straight All-Star Games

~ Cal extends his streak to 927 games and 8,243 innings

Season Stats

	YEAR	CAREER
Average	.252	.283
Games	162	992
At Bats	624	3834
Runs	97	626
Hits	157	1084
Doubles	28	211
Triples	3	23
Home Runs	27	160
RBI	98	570
Bases on Balls	81	394
Strikeouts	77	494
Stolen Bases	3	14
Errors	20	125

THE YEAR THAT WAS – 1987

The L.A. Lakers defeat the Boston Celtics in the NBA Championship.

Milwaukee wins its 13th straight game to start the season, setting a new AL record for the most successful start.

On May 14: Cal surpasses Nellie Fox and becomes ninth on the all-time consecutive games played list.

The Grammy Award for best album goes to U2 for The Joshua Tree.

On June 16: Cal ties Eddie Yost for seventh on the all-time consecutive games played list while also picking up his 1,000th hit as the Orioles lose 6-5 to the Yankees in New York.

Former member of the group Wham!, George Michael has the #1 Billboard hit of the year – "Faith."

On July 11: Cal's brother Billy Ripken makes his ML debut as Cal's double play partner at second base. They become the 5th set of brothers to form a second base/shortstop combination in ML history. Although the Orioles lost that night, they would win their next 11 games with the brother combination.

Oliver Stone's highly acclaimed Platoon wins Best Picture.

The Cosby Show reigns as the most talked about and popular show.

Cal gets ejected for the first time in his career in the bottom of the 1st inning after arguing a strike call with the home plate umpire, Tim Welke, in a game vs. New York at Memorial Stadium.

Cal and Kelly prepare for their November wedding.

The '87 World Series showcases the Twins and the Cardinals with the Twins victorious.

"Black Monday" marks the end of the bull market, when Wall Street experiences its three biggest one-day point losses ever.

1988

Ripken Season Milestones

~ Is the co-winner with Eddie Murray for "Most Valuable Oriole" Award

~ Leads American League shortstops in putouts (284)

~ Extends streak to 1,088 games

~ Leads major league shortstops in home runs and RBI

Season Stats

	YEAR	CAREER
Average	.264	.280
Games	161	1153
At Bats	575	4409
Runs	87	713
Hits	152	1236
Doubles	25	236
Triples	1	24
Home Runs	23	183
RBI	81	651
Bases on Balls	102	496
Strikeouts	69	563
Stolen Bases	2	16
Errors	21	146

THE YEAR THAT WAS – 1988

The Washington Redskins defeat the Denver Broncos in the Super Bowl.

The L.A. Lakers defeat the Detroit Pistons in the NBA Championship.

The Oscar winner for 1988 is The Last Emperor.

The Grammy Award for best album is Faith by George Michael.

Cal Ripken, Jr. SS

June 25: In game 1,000 of Cal's streak, he goes 2 for 4 with a 2-run homer off Bruce Hurst in a loss to the Red Sox in Boston.

The #1 song on the Billboard chart is INXS's "Need You Tonight."

Stefan Edberg wins the men's Wimbledon final and Steffi Graf is the ladies' champion.

Who Framed Roger Rabbit?, Willow, The Presidio, Crocodile Dundee II and that all-time favorite baseball movie, Bull Durham, are hot at the box office.

The Cosby Show still covets first place in television ratings.

The 1988 World Series features the Minnesota Twins and the St. Louis Cardinals. The Twins win.

1989

CALVIN EDWIN RIPKEN JR.

Ripken Season Milestones

~ Leads major league shortstops in home runs and RBI

~ Has career-high 47 consecutive errorless game streak (239tc)

~ Is named "the smartest player" in the American League in a *Toronto Sun* survey of managers

~ Wins his fifth "Silver Slugger" award

~ Is named to three All-Star teams (AP major league, *USA Today*, and *The Sporting News*)

~ Leads the club in hits (166), doubles (30), and RBI (93)

Season Stats

	YEAR	CAREER
Average	.257	.277
Games	162	1315
At Bats	646	5055
Runs	80	793
Hits	166	1402
Doubles	30	266
Triples	0	24
Home Runs	21	204
RBI	93	744
Bases on Balls	57	553
Strikeouts	72	635
Stolen Bases	3	19
Errors	8	154

THE YEAR THAT WAS – 1989

The San Francisco 49ers defeat the Cincinnati Bengals in the Super Bowl.

The Detroit Pistons defeat the L.A. Lakers in the NBA Championship.

The Cosby Show is still number one; however, Super Bowl XXIII is the most watched television event of the year.

May 8: Cal surpasses Billy Williams, as he becomes fourth on the all-time consecutive games played list when the O's play the A's in Baltimore.

Boris Becker and Steffi Graf win Wimbledon.

The Grammy Award for best album goes to Bonnie Raitt for Nick of Time.

Dustin Hoffman and Tom Cruise star in this year's hit directed by Baltimore native Barry Levinson – the Oscar winning Rainman.

August 9: Cal plays in game #1,200 at Memorial Stadium.

August 17: In Game #1,208, Cal celebrates surpassing Steve Garvey to become number three on the all-time consecutive games played list by going 3 for 5 with a 2-run homer in an O's 11-6 win at Detroit.

The #1 Billboard song of the year is "Another Day in Paradise" by Phil Collins.

Cal extends his streak to 1,250.

The Oakland Athletics defeat the San Francisco Giants in the World Series.

November 22: Cal and Kelly's first child, Rachel Marie, is born.

Cal Ripken SS

Ripken Passes Garvey, Celebrates With Ho-Hum

1990

Ripken Season Milestones

~ Cal wins the Lou Hatter Most Valuable Oriole award outright for the first time after sharing it with Eddie Murray twice before

~ Cal creates an all-time standard for consistency at shortstop by committing only three errors in 161 games for a major league record percentage of .996

~ Cal becomes the most prolific home run-hitting shortstop in American League history — Cal breaks the 20 barrier in home runs for the ninth straight year, extending his major league record for shortstops

Season Stats

	YEAR	CAREER
Average	.250	.274
Games	161	1476
At Bats	600	5655
Runs	78	871
Hits	150	1552
Doubles	28	294
Triples	4	28
Home Runs	21	225
RBI	84	828
Bases on Balls	82	635
Strikeouts	66	701
Stolen Bases	3	22
Errors	3	154

THE YEAR THAT WAS – 1990

In the NBA Championship, the Detroit Pistons defeat the Portland Trail Blazers.

The San Francisco 49ers defeat the Denver Broncos in the 1990 Super Bowl.

Jessica Tandy and Morgan Freeman capture the Academy's hearts in the Oscar Award-Winning film Driving Miss Daisy.

Cal plays in his 1,300th game in New York going 1 for 3 as the O's defeat the Yankees in New York.

June 12: Cal surpasses Everett Scott to become 2nd to Lou Gehrig on the all-time consecutive game streak. The Orioles defeated the Milwaukee Brewers 4-3 at home that day when Randy Milligan hit a solo homer leading off the bottom of the 10th.

The Grammy Award-Winning Album is Quincy Jones's Back on the Block.

Cal's record streak of 95 errorless games ends.

Cal is elected as the American League's All-Star starting shortstop for the seventh straight year, a league record. Cal extends his streak to 1,411.

Winbledon champions are Stefan Edberg and Martina Navratilova.

The Cincinnati Reds defeat the Oakland Athletics in the World Series.

Ripken is voted to record 7th All-Star start in row

CAL RIPKEN, JR. SS

1991

CALVIN EDWIN RIPKEN JR.

Ripken Season Milestones

~ Cal becomes the second player in major league history to win a league Most Valuable Player, Major League Player of the Year, All-Star Game MVP, and a Gold Glove in the same season

~ Cal wins his sixth "Silver Slugger" award

~ Cal wins his first Rawlings Gold Glove

~ Cal becomes the fourth shortstop in major league history to hit 30 or more home runs

~ Cal leads the majors in road batting average (.358)

~ Cal leads major league shortstops in total chances (807), assists (529), and putouts (267)

Season Stats

	YEAR	CAREER
Average	.323	.279
Games	162	1638
At Bats	650	6305
Runs	99	970
Hits	210	1762
Doubles	46	340
Triples	5	33
Home Runs	34	259
RBI	114	942
Bases on Balls	53	688
Strikeouts	46	747
Stolen Bases	6	28
Errors	11	165

THE YEAR THAT WAS – 1991

Brooks: Gold Glove has fit Ripken for years

Kevin Costner's Dances With Wolves sweeps at the Academy Awards, winning Best Picture and Best Musical Score.

The Chicago Bulls defeat the L.A. Lakers in the NBA Championship.

The New York Giants defeat the Buffalo Bills in the Super Bowl.

The Grammy Award-Winning Album of the year is Natalie Cole's Unforgettable.

At that point in the Streak (1,500 consecu-tive games, all starts) Cal had been removed from a game just 29 times. At 1,500 consecutive games, Lou Gehrig had not played a complete game 47 times (45 early outs and 2 no-starts).

The #1 Billboard single is "(Everything I Do) I Do It For You" by Bryan Adams from the Robin Hood Soundtrack.

Game 1,500 of The Streak: Before the game, Cal is presented with the Chevrolet All-Star Game MVP trophy (2 for 3 with a 2-run homer off Dennis Martinez on July 9 in Toronto) in front of the Memorial Stadium crowd of 39,384. He then went on to play in his 1,500th consecutive game, going 1 for 4 with a 2-run homer off Seattle's Rich DeLucia in the O's 4-1 win.

Cheers is the favorite American television show of the year.

Cal was 30 years old at game #1,500: Lou Gehrig was 31 when he played in his 1,500th game on September 25, 1934 at Philadelphia (he hit his 48th homer of the season that day).

Ripken's homer that night was his 20th of the sea-son. With that, he became the 8th player all-time to hit 20+ homers in his first 10 full seasons.

The Minnesota Twins defeat the Atlanta Braves in the World Series.

1992

CALVIN EDWIN RIPKEN JR

Ripken Season Milestones

~ Cal wins his second consecutive Rawlings Gold Glove Award

~ Cal becomes the Orioles all-time greatest home run hitter

~ Cal is named the recipient of the Roberto Clemente Award

~ Cal is named 38th winner of the annual Lou Gehrig
Memorial Award

~ Cal extends his streak to 1,735 games

Season Stats

	YEAR	CAREER
Average	.251	.277
Games	162	1800
At Bats	637	6942
Runs	73	1043
Hits	160	1922
Doubles	29	369
Triples	1	34
Home Runs	14	273
RBI	72	1014
Bases on Balls	64	752
Strikeouts	50	797
Stolen Bases	4	32
Errors	12	177

THE YEAR THAT WAS - 1992

The Washington Redskins defeat the Buffalo Bills in the Super Bowl.

In the 1992 NBA Championship, the Chicago Bulls defeat the Portland Trail Blazers.

A California jury acquits four white Los Angeles police officers of beating black motorist Rodney King, after the videotape was broadcast around the world.

Billboards #1 song of the year is "I Will Always Love You" by Whitney Houston.

Ripken's fielding Golden again

At Wimbledon, Andre Agassi and Steffi Graf are the winners.

Album of the Year belongs to Eric Clapton for Unplugged.

August 24: Prior to the game (Cal's 32nd birthday), Cal signs a 5-year 30.5 million dollar contract that runs through the '97 season.

Anthony Hopkins and Jodie Foster chilled audiences with their film The Silence of the Lambs.

60 Minutes ranks as the top show of the year.

VISàVIS

The Toronto Blue Jays defeat the Atlanta Braves in the World Series.

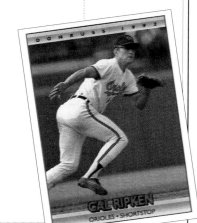

CAL RIPKEN
ORIOLES · SHORTSTOP

1993

Ripken Season Milestones

~ Cal leads ML shortstops in home runs for the ninth time in 11 years

~ Cal leads AL shortstops in assists (495) and total chances (738)

~ Cal becomes the top home run-hitting shortstop in major league history (278)

~ Cal receives a career-high 19 intentional walks

~ Cal appears in his 11th All-Star Game, his 10th start

~ Cal extends his streak to 1,897 games

Season Stats

	YEAR	CAREER
Average	.257	.275
Games	162	1962
At Bats	641	7583
Runs	87	1130
Hits	165	2087
Doubles	26	395
Triples	3	37
Home Runs	24	297
RBI	90	1104
Bases on Balls	65	817
Strikeouts	58	855
Stolen Bases	1	33
Errors	17	194

THE YEAR THAT WAS – 1993

The Dallas Cowboys defeat the Buffalo Bills in the Super Bowl.

In the NBA Championship, the Chicago Bulls defeat the Phoenix Suns.

Cult leader David Koresh and many of his followers die in a Texas compound fire.

The Grammy Award-Winning album of the year is Whitney Houston's The Bodyguard.

A hit song, and a popular tune in ballparks and arenas is The Tag Team's "Whoomp, There It Is!"

Clint Eastwood directs and stars in the Oscar-winning picture Unforgiven.

Cal plays in his 11th All-Star Game at Oriole Park at Camden Yards – his hometown.

At Wimbledon, Pete Sampras wins his first of four championships; Steffi Graf wins the women's again.

The Ripkens' second child, Ryan Calvin, is born.

60 Minutes ranks as the top show of the year; Super Bowl XXVII is the most watched event of the year.

The Toronto Blue Jays defeat the Philadelphia Phillies in the World Series.

CAL RIPKEN, JR. 8

1994

CALVIN EDWIN RIPKEN JR

Ripken Season Milestones

~ Leads major league shortstops in fielding percentage (.985)

~ Leads the American League with 46 multi-hit games

~ Extends his major league record for most consecutive games by a shortstop to 1,982

~ Establishes the major league record for most years leading the league in double plays by a shortstop to seven

~ Leads AL Shortstops with 13 home runs

Season Stats

	YEAR	CAREER
Average	.315	.277
Games	112	2009
At Bats	444	8027
Runs	71	1201
Hits	140	2227
Doubles	19	414
Triples	3	40
Home Runs	13	310
RBI	75	1179
Bases on Balls	32	849
Strikeouts	41	896
Stolen Bases	1	34
Errors	7	201

THE YEAR THAT WAS – 1994

The Cowboys beat the Bills in the Super Bowl.

The Houston Rockets defeat the New York Knicks in the NBA Championship.

Forrest Gump sweeps the Oscars. It wins Best Picture, Best Actor (Tom Hanks), and Best Director.

The British pop group Ace of Base has the #1 Billboard song, "The Sign."

At Wimbledon, Pete Sampras and Conchita Martinez are the champions.

The Grammy Award-winning album of the year belongs to Cheryl Crow.

July 31: Cal plays in Game 1,999 at home: Due to two canceled games just two weeks earlier in Seattle because of falling acoustic tiles at the Kingdome, Cal plays consecutive game #1,999 in Baltimore on the last day of a homestand, thus denying him the chance to break #2,000 at home. A full-house crowd of 47,684 gave Cal a standing ovation when he took the field in the top of the fourth. The game wound up being the last home contest for the O's in '94 due to the strike.

Cal plays in his 2,000th consecutive game on August 1 in Minnesota.

There is no World Series due to a strike which ended the baseball season in August.

Cal plays more games at shortstop than any other Oriole in history.

Home Improvement, Seinfeld, and Friends are the talk of TV.

On Election Day, the Republicans win a resounding victory by taking control of both houses of Congress for the first time in 40 years.

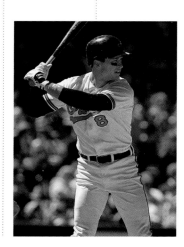

1995

Ripken Season Milestones

~ Becomes O's All-Time runs leader with his second run of the night on July 4th vs. Minnesota

~ Hits his fourth career grand slam on Saturday, June 3rd off Oakland's Mike Harkey

~ Plays in his 13th consecutive All-Star game in Arlington, Texas

~ Hits two home runs in one game on July 31st against Toronto for the 14th time in his career

~ Played in his 2,100th consecutive game on August 5th at home

Season Stats

Average	.260
Games	109
At Bats	419
Runs	49
Hits	109
Doubles	26
Triples	2
Home Runs	12
RBI	60
Bases on Balls	36
Strikeouts	47
Stolen Bases	0
Errors	7

AS OF AUGUST 23, 1995

THE YEAR THAT WAS – 1995

The Oklahoma City bombing draws national attention as people all over the country respond to the horrible incident.

Michael Jackson's much anticipated compact disc is released: History: Past, Present, and Future.

After being arrested for soliciting a prostitute in Los Angeles, Hugh Grant's movie Nine Months does well at the box office.

June 3: vs. Oakland: Cal hits a grand slam during an afternoon game at Oriole Park as the Birds defeat the Oakland A's 9–5.

Kevin Costner makes the most expensive movie ever: Waterworld.

The Whitewater hearings begin in Washington, D.C.

Hootie and the Blowfish's Cracked Rear View is the biggest album of the year.

President Clinton moves to tighten the laws regarding under-aged smoking.

Cal becomes a spokesperson for Adventure World and Coca-Cola.

The Cal Sessions

1995 HAS BEEN AN EXCITING — and incredibly busy — year for Cal Ripken Jr. Thus far, he's played every game of yet another season, signed countless autographs before and after ballgames and spoken to the media at various press conferences in major league cities about The Streak. Time and time again, he graciously takes questions from the press. The same questions are often asked over and over again. It can quickly become tedious and mundane, but Cal continues to smile and answer them.

He is a unique individual and handles the pressures of professional baseball like it's old hat. In a sense, it may be because he knows the ins and outs and ups and downs of baseball so well. He enjoys playing and welcomes the daily challenge it poses.

What follows are excerpts from the many media sessions held this season, questions posed by reporters and answered by the Iron Man himself. He has answered them many times over, and his replies are always the same. And always heartfelt.

Q: Barring any rain outs, you'd tie the record September 5th and break it at home on the 6th. Do you have anything special planned for that day with the family?

A: I'm someone that doesn't look too far ahead. It's hard enough just to stay focused on a day to day level. I have no plans. I'm thinking about tonight's game and when tonight's game is over, I'll think about tomorrow. It's my only way to protect myself and allow myself to go out and do the things that I've done all these years. It's just my own way of dealing with it. I don't know any other way. I try to block out those kinds of questions. I try not to think too far ahead; just try to concentrate on the here and now. That's the best way I know to handle it.

Q: *Cal, how comfortable are you, if at all, with the game of baseball and where it's going?*

A: There have been a lot of troubles, especially recently, with baseball overall. My way of dealing with it is really to accentuate the positive. Focus on the beauty of the game, why we like the game and maybe on all of the positives. If this accomplishment is a positive for baseball, I think that's good. I don't feel any additional burden or responsibility. I'm just going to try to do what I do. I think that there are so many positive things in baseball itself; if we really want to look to see them, then we'll see them. If we really try to accentuate those positive things then you'll find out why we like baseball so much: because of the beauty of the game. And it is the players a little bit, but it is the game itself that stays. The players come through, play and make their mark, and then there are new players that come in. My belief is that baseball is the greatest game and there are so may positive things about it.

Q: *As you get older, you know a little bit more about the game and how to play the batters better and you are in the right place at the right time more often. Is this true?*

A: Generally speaking, as you get older, you lose a little bit of your physical talent. There's no doubt about it that you are not as resilient as you used to be. You don't hit the ball as far or as hard. You cannot throw the ball as well. But what you lose a little bit in your skill level, you gain in experience. You know how to play the game better and you know where to play. Therefore, if you add up all of those things, you're a better player. At some point, you lose too much skill, and your experience can't make up for it. That's the time for you to leave. People will let you know that's the time for you to leave.

Q: *People now associate you so much with The Streak that they forget that in 1983 you won a World's Championship and were the MVP that year. Does 1983 seem like a long time ago?*

A: Very long ago, yes. I came to the big leagues and had a chance to establish myself as an everyday player on a very good team and we won. My first year we went to the last set of the season before we lost to Milwaukee, which was a really exciting season and made for an exciting weekend. And the next year we went on to win the World Series. Looking back on it, I think that maybe I had taken that for granted too much. I was in my second year. I was young and trying to get everything going. All of a sudden, you win the World Series. I think that it's been a long time and I've never been back...never been back to the playoffs. I think if I had the opportunity to go back to the playoffs or to the World Series now, I'd be in a position to appreciate it a whole lot more this time having gone through 0-21 starts, having gone through losing a 100 and some games.

When I first came to the big leagues, I thought that after the first two years, it was going to be the same throughout my whole career, but because it hasn't and because we have lost and because I have endured a rebuilding process, I'd love to get back to the World Series and feel that feeling again.

Q: What's the closest point in The Streak when you came to losing it, when you thought that maybe you wouldn't be able to play tomorrow?

A: There have been two physical injuries that had a real impact. The one was a long, long time ago. It was 1985 early in the season. I sprained my ankle on a pick-off play at second base. I remember that Gary Ward was the runner and Mike Boddicker was the pitcher. I caught my spikes on top of the bag and turned my ankle. It was a Wednesday afternoon game and I think that I taped it up tight, finished the game. Then, after the game was over, it blew up. We had an off-day Thursday and a Friday night game. I had a full day and a half to get the swelling down. If I would have had to play on Thursday, I don't think that I could have played. But, as it turned out, Friday it way okay and Saturday, it was a little bit better and as I played on it, it seemed to get better. The other one — I had a little knee injury on that Seattle brawl that we had two years ago. I was running in one direction, lost my footing, tried to turn, twisted my knee, and I wasn't sure whether I would be able to play the next game. When I woke up, I was pretty convinced that I would not be able to play. As the day wore on — as luck would have it — it loosened up. When I got to the ballpark, I tested it and I felt that I could go out and play. That's what I did and it got better.

Q: Tell us about your work ethic? Who has been most influential?

A: My approach to the game has probably been influenced all by my father. Essentially, in a team game like baseball is, your teammates rely on you to be in the line-up every day. From the very beginning, my dad preached that it was

Top Ten Consecutive Game Streaks

PLAYER	
1. Lou Gehrig	2,130
2. CAL RIPKEN JR	2,119
3. Everett Scott	1,307
4. Steve Garvey	1,207
5. Billy Williams	1,117
6. Joe Sewell	1,103
7. Stan Musial	895
8. Eddie Yost	829
9. Gus Suhr	822
10. Nellie Fox	798

AS OF AUGUST 23, 1995

Home Runs (1982-1995)

PLAYER	
1. Eddie Murray	340
2. Andre Dawson	324
3. CAL RIPKEN JR	322
4. Joe Carter	321
5. Dale Murphy	306

AS OF AUGUST 23, 1995

Runs Batted In (1982-1995)

PLAYER	
1. Eddie Murray	1,317
2. CAL RIPKEN JR	1,239
3. Andre Dawson	1,180
4. Joe Carter	1,159
5. Harold Baines	1,157

AS OF AUGUST 23, 1995

At Bats
(1982-1995)

PLAYER

1. CAL RIPKEN JR   8,407
2. Eddie Murray   7,655
3. Wade Boggs   7,483
4. Tim Wallach   7,454
5. Ryne Sandberg   7,378

AS OF AUGUST 23, 1995

Hits
(1982-1995)

PLAYER

1. Wade Boggs   2,500
2. Tony Gwynn   2,343
3. CAL RIPKEN JR   2,331
4. Kirby Puckett   2,266
5. Ryne Sandberg   2,132

AS OF AUGUST 23, 1995

Runs
(1982-1995)

PLAYER

1. Rickey Henderson 1,454
2. Tim Raines   1,288
3. Wade Boggs   1,265
4. CAL RIPKEN JR   1,249
5. Paul Molitor   1,248

AS OF AUGUST 23, 1995

important to be there, in the line-up, on a daily basis. Maybe I've exaggerated the point a little bit, but I still think it's important to go out there and play in a baseball season 162 games. You can help your team win in the first inning by turning a double play or guessing right on a hit and run and if the coverage was right and you avoid a bad beginning. It's just always been preached to me to be out there every day. My father is the one who has turned me in that direction.

Q: As you approach this milestone, another milestone has been reached by your former teammate, Eddie Murray. Can you comment on what it was like to play with him?

A: Eddie was a great friend, a great teammate. I think he's one of the greatest clutch-hitters that I ever played with. He made my job a whole lot easier. When I was hitting third in front of Eddie, you knew when the game was on the line that your job wasn't to win the game, your job was to put the bat into his hands so that he could win the game. Those types of players are very rare. He probably taught me first-hand the importance of playing every day, the importance of being in the line-up...the stability that you provide offensively and defensively. I just remember that Eddie played almost every single game. He showed me that it was important to play through all sorts of injuries. My approach was formulated through my dad and through his teachings early on, but I actually saw someone put those teachings to work. Eddie was a really big influence on knowing how important it is to play every day.

Q: Has The Streak affected your privacy? Has that changed you at all?

A: It's understood, as the game of baseball has grown as an entertainment format, that you are on duty a whole lot more. The accomplishments you have and your notoriety is going to be bigger. Maybe your face will be recognized a little bit more; therefore some of these things will happen. It's just a matter of trying to deal with it. We are all different people and sometimes when you come to the ballpark and you play every day, you know that there's going to be a lot going on. When I'm away from it, I try to refuel. I need the time and space for myself. I really favor my own privacy for that reason, because I need to regroup so that I can come out here and deal with it every single day. I'm a private person, but I realize that when you are in the public and you are out here playing baseball, that you have to be more of a public figure.

Q: *Have you noticed that some people are taking The Streak for granted?*

A: I actually appreciate the fact that it's been taken for granted. I'm not someone who really likes to sit down and talk about it a lot. I don't put a certain level of importance on it that maybe some other people do. It's simple to me that I've been lucky that I was able to establish myself as an everyday player early. The manager wanted to put me in there. And, I've stayed away from any serious injuries, so now all of a sudden you go out there every day and do whatever you can and the next day comes and you want to play. Then you look up ten, eleven, twelve, thirteen years later, and you are in this situation. I'm kind of glad, at least from a perspective, that I have to deal with it and manage it every day. I'm glad that people just seem to let it flow. Maybe it's the way that I've handled it and kind of downplayed it and not talked about it. Maybe that's the reason it's gone the way it has.

Q: *It wasn't long ago that people were saying that this was probably the most untouchable, unbreakable record. Do you think that it's an unbreakable record?*

A: I don't think so. I've never really thought in terms of records. I know as kids, we look at records and we dream and we think that maybe someday you'd have a chance to hit so many home runs. But, once you start getting into it and see some of the things like 60 home runs in a year and 56-game hitting streaks and 755 home runs and those kinds of things, you know that they are there and you think that they are unattainable. Then comes someone like Ken Griffey Jr. or Matt Williams who's on a pace to hit 60 home runs. So you realize that maybe it is possible. In my situation, I never set out to do this. It hasn't been a lifelong dream of mine. I don't know what to make of it. If you had asked me ten years ago I would have said it was inconceivable at the time. But, by going out and playing every day and you stay away from injuries, your name is still in the line-up. Then you look up and say, I don't know how, but I'm here and I'm going to keep doing what I'm doing.

Q: *We paint you as a "throw back" ballplayer of old. Is this a true thing or not? Are you a great deal different than the people that you are playing with right now?*

A: I don't think so. I think that we all share the same energy and the same desire. When you are on the baseball field, there is real equality. We all wanted to be ballplayers since we started playing as kids, not when we first started professional ball. All of the hours that you put into practice, all of the leagues that you play

Extra Base Hits (1982-1994)

PLAYER

1.	CAL RIPKEN JR	804
2.	Eddie Murray	742
3.	Andre Dawson	741
4.	Joe Carter	702
5.	Dave Winfield	670

AS OF AUGUST 23, 1995

Doubles (1982-1994)

PLAYER

1.	Wade Boggs	480
2.	CAL RIPKEN JR	440
3.	Don Mattingly	434
4.	Tim Wallach	407
5.	George Brett	394

AS OF AUGUST 23, 1995

Orioles All-Time Games

PLAYER

1. Brooks Robinson 2,986
2. CAL RIPKEN JR 2,183
3. Mark Belanger 1,962
4. Eddie Murray 1,820
5. Boog Powell 1,763

AS OF AUGUST 23, 1995

Orioles All-Time Hits

PLAYER

1. Brooks Robinson 2,848
2. CAL RIPKEN JR 2,336
3. Eddie Murray 2,021
4. Boog Powell 1,574
5. Ken Singleton 1,455

AS OF AUGUST 23, 1995

Orioles All-Time Home Runs

PLAYER

1. Eddie Murray 333
2. CAL RIPKEN JR 322
3. Boog Powell 303
4. Brooks Robinson 268
5. Ken Singleton 182

AS OF AUGUST 23, 1995

in, all the work that it takes to get to this level. I think that everyone shares that same desire and that same feeling about the game. I don't know why I am looked at as a "throw back." I know that I had a set of experiences that maybe most other players did not. I grew up in professional baseball. I grew up with my dad in the minor leagues and getting to go to the ballpark all the time, talking to players, listening, watching, getting instruction. That kind of exposure helps you fully understand the game.

Q: Have you ever missed a game in high school or Little League?

A: I didn't have perfect attendance in school. I missed a few games in Little League. I never missed any games in high school because of injury I don't think, but I missed them in the minor leagues.

Q: How do you and Lou Gehrig compare?

A: I try very hard not to think about that. The only comparison you can make between Lou Gehrig as a player and me as a player is that we have The Streak in common. Other than that, he was a far better hitter than I'll ever be, probably a far better player than I'll ever be. I've tried not to learn about him. I've tried not to think about him because I just want to be me and play the game and do everything I believe is right. Then, when the game is over, I'll look back and say, 'I did everything I could' and be satisfied with my effort.

Q: Have you gone out and maybe studied up on the writings of Lou Gehrig and his streak?

A: As a baseball fan, of course I'm curious about every baseball player, but Lou Gehrig? I'm a little fearful of learning about him, only because my approach is genuine. My approach is how I was taught. I'm fearful that if I start learning about Lou Gehrig, I'll start to be obsessed with the idea of The Streak. That's counter-productive to me. I don't want to be obsessed with it. People have given me a book or an article or a baseball card or any number of things about Lou Gehrig thinking that since we have this streak in common, that it's natural and I'd want to know about it. I'm curious, but I put them away in a box and after my days are over or after this whole thing is over, I'll sit down and look at it from a baseball fan's perspective. That's how I look at it.

Q: The Hall of Fame. Do you ever think about it someday?

A: Absolutely not. ■

Acknowledgments

EDITOR

Stephanie Parrillo

ASSOCIATE EDITOR

Bill Stetka

BUSINESS MANAGER

Bob Gallion

DESIGN AND PRODUCTION

Beshara Associates, Inc.

SPECIAL THANKS TO

Spiro Alafassos, Patricia Bateman, Margaret Benkard, Stephen Beshara, Jason
Brenner, Joe Foss, Walt Gutowski, John Maroon, Paul McNeeley, Jenny Scott,
Heather Tilles, Carey Vizzi, Chris Voxakis, Sam Voxakis, and Marcy Zerhusen

PRINCIPAL PHOTOGRAPHY

Jerry Wachter and Scott Wachter

ADDITIONAL PHOTOGRAPHY

Greg Abramowitz, F.O.S. Inc., Ray Gilbert, Erik Kvalsvik, Mitchell Layton,
Norma McNair, National Baseball Hall of Fame Library, Tom Sullivan,
Mort Tadder, and Jo Winstead

THANKS TO THE FOLLOWING PUBLICATIONS FOR COVER REPRINTS

Baseball America, Baseball Card News, Sports Illustrated, Topps Magazine,
and Vis-A-Vis Magazine

PRINTER

French Bray, Inc.